Piano/Vocal

The Judy Garland
Souvenir Songbook

68 Songs
•
Photos
•
Movie Stills
•
Film Facts
•
Filmography
•
Discography

Harold –
Let's always go
'Over the Rainbow'
together –
love
Judy

Photo: Courtesy of Harold Arlen

The Judy Garland
Souvenir Songbook

Compiled and Edited by

Howard Harnne

ISBN 0-88188-390-5

HAL•LEONARD®
CORPORATION

7777 W. BLUEMOUND RD. P.O. BOX 13819 MILWAUKEE, WI 53213

Visit Hal Leonard on the internet at http://www.halleonard.com

Contents

Film Facts (Chronologically) & Featured Songs from Films

Alphabetical Song Guide to the Collection

JUDY GARLAND:
IN MOVIES AND SONGS

"She is a star; the genuine outsize article. . . . She is an actress of power and subtlety;
A singer whose way with a song is nothing short of marvelous. . . . She is a great artist.
She is Judy. She is the best there is."

Phillip Oakes, London Critic

EVERY SUNDAY (1936), MGM
Directed by Felix Feist
with Judy Garland as Judy, Deanna Durbin and Sid Silvers
Judy sang *"Americana"*, and a verse to it by Roger Edens
("Waltz with a Swing")

Judy with Deanna Durbin in "EVERY SUNDAY"

Anthony Martin and *Judy* in "PIGSKIN PARADE"

PIGSKIN PARADE (1936), 20th Century-Fox
 Directed by David Butler
 Associate Producer Bogart Rogers
 Screenplay by Harry Tugend, Jack Yellen and William Conselman
 Original Story by Art Sheekman, Nat Perrin and Mark Kelly
 Musical Direction by David Buttolph
 Costumes by Gwen Wakeling
 Photography by Arthur Miller
 Film Editing by Irene Morra
 CAST
  Stuart Erwin, Patsy Kelly, Jack Haley, The Yacht Club Boys, Johnny Downs, Betty Grable,
  Arline Judge, Dixie Dunbar, Judy Garland (as Sairy Dodd), Anthony "Tony" Martin, Grady
  Sutton, Fred Kohler, Jr., Elisha Cook, Jr., Eddie Nugent, Julius Tannen, Pat Flaherty, Si Jenks,
  Lynn Bari, George Offerman, Jr., Maurice Cass, Douglas Wood, Alan Ladd.

 JUDY'S SONGS - All written by Sidney Mitchell & Lew Pollack
  It's Love I'm After
  The Balboa
  The Texas Tornado
  Hold That Bulldog (cut before release)

BROADWAY MELODY OF 1938 (1937) - MGM

Directed by Roy Del Ruth
Produced by Jack Cummings
Screenplay by Jack McGowan
Original Story by Jack McGowan and Sid Silvers
Music and Lyrics by Nacio Herb Brown and Arthur Freed
Dance Direction by Dave Gould
Musical Direction by George Stoll
Arrangements by Roger Edens
Costumes by Adrian
Photography by William Daniels
Film Editing by Blanche Sewell
Art Direction by Cedric Gibbons

CAST
Robert Taylor, Eleanor Powell, George Murphy, Binnie Barnes, Buddy Ebsen, Sophie Tucker,
Judy Garland (as Betty Clayton), Charles Igor Gorin, Raymond Walburn, Robert Benchley,
Willie Howard, Esther Howard, Grace Hayle, Billy Gilbert, Charles Grapewin, Robert Wildhack,
Barnett Parker, Helen Troy.
JUDY'S SONGS
(Dear Mr. Gable) You Made Me Love You
Everybody Sing
Yours and Mine
Finale

Judy and her audience in "BROADWAY MELODY OF 1938"

You Made Me Love You
(I Didn't Want to Do It)

Words by JOE McCARTHY
Music by JAMES V. MONACO

6

and I thought I'd write and tell you so._____

Slowly

You Made Me Love You, I did-n't wan-na do it, I

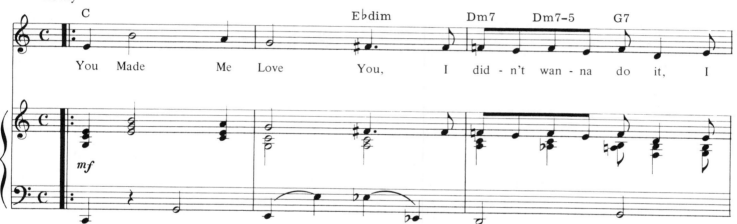

did-n't wan-na do it, You made me want you, and all the time you knew it,

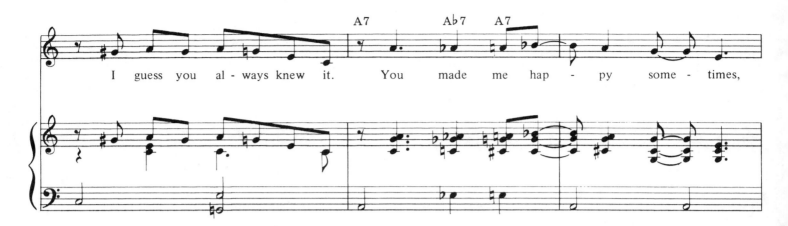

I guess you al-ways knew it. You made me hap-py some-times,

you made me glad,___ But there were times,___ dear, you made___

___ me feel so bad.___ You made me sigh for, I

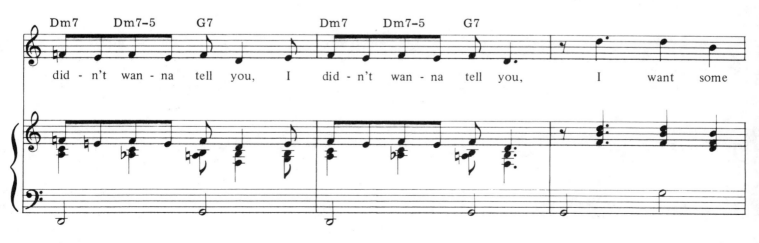

did-n't wan-na tell you, I did-n't wan-na tell you, I want some

9

Freddie Bartholomew and *Judy* in "LISTEN, DARLING"

LISTEN, DARLING (1938) - MGM

Produced by Jack Cummings
Directed by Edwin L. Marin
Screenplay by Elaine Ryan and Anne Morrison Chapin
Original Story by Katherine Brush
Musical Direction by George Stoll
Arrangements by Roger Edens
Music and Lyrics by Joseph McCarthy, Milton Ager, Al Lewis,
     Al Hoffman, Murray Mencher and James Hanley
Costumes by Dolly Tree
Photography by Charles Lawton, Jr.
Art Direction by Cedric Gibbons
Film Editing by Blanche Sewell

CAST

Freddie Bartholomew, Judy Garland (as Pinkie Wingate), Mary Astor, Walter Pidgeon, Alan Hale, Charley Grapewin, Scotty Beckett, Gene Lockhart, Barnett Parker, Byron Foulger, Bobbie Stebbins

JUDY'S SONGS

Zing! Went the Strings of My Heart
Ten Pins in the Sky
On the Bumpy Road to Love

Zing! Went the Strings of My Heart

Words and Music by JAMES F. HANLEY

All na - ture seemed to be

In per - fect har - mo - ny,__ Zing! Went The Strings Of My Heart.___

___ Your eyes made skies seem blue a - gain, What else could I do a - gain, But

keep re - peat - ing through a - gain, "I love you, love you!"

Judy and Mickey Rooney in "THOROUGHBREDS DON'T CRY"

THOROUGHBREDS DON'T CRY (1937) · MGM
Produced by Harry Rapf
Directed by Alfred E. Green
Screenplay by Lawrence Hazard
Original Story by Eleanore Griffin and J. Walter Ruben
Music and Lyrics by Nacio Herb Brown and Arthur Freed
Musical Direction by William Axt
Costumes by Dolly Tree
Photography by Leonard Smith
Film Editing by Elmo Vernon
CAST
    Judy Garland (as Cricket West), Mickey Rooney, Sophie Tucker, C. Aubrey Smith, Ronald
    Sinclair, Helen Troy, Forrester Harvey, Frankie Darro, Charles D. Brown, Henry Kolker.
JUDY'S SONGS
    Got a Pair of New Shoes
    Sun Showers (cut before release)

SING, JUDY GARLAND!

You've got the whole world singing with you in your new hit! Cheers for Judy as she soars to stardom on the wings of melody and mirth.

It's 1938's first all-star spectacular triumph!

FANNY BRICE

"BABY SNOOKS" on the screen at last! Radio's new comic sensation is a panic in the movies!

ALLAN JONES

The star of "The Firefly" sings and romances as never before ... new tunes to sing ... and Lynne Carver for inspiration!

Everybody Sing

and

REGINALD OWEN · BILLIE BURKE
REGINALD GARDINER
LYNNE CARVER

Original Story and Screen Play by Florence Ryerson and Edgar Allan Woolf. Additional Dialogue by James Gruen

Directed by EDWIN L. MARIN

Produced by HARRY RAPF

A Metro-Goldwyn-Mayer Picture

Lynne Carver, *Judy,* Reginald Gardiner and Allan Jones in "EVERYBODY SING"

EVERYBODY SING (1938) - MGM
    Produced by Harry Rapf
    Directed by Edwin L. Marin
    Screenplay by Florence Ryerson and Edgar Woolf
    Original Story by Florence Ryerson and Edgar Allan Woolf
    Additional Dialogue by James Gruen
    Musical Arrangements by Roger Edens
    Music and Lyrics by Gus Kahn, Bronislau Kaper, Walter Jurmann,
        Harry Ruby and Bert Kalmar
    Costumes by Dolly Tree
    Photography by Joseph Ruttenberg
CAST
    Allan Jones, Fanny Brice, Judy Garland (as Judy Bellaire), Billie Burke, Lynne Carver, Reginald
    Owen, Reginald Gardiner, Helen Troy, Monty Woolley, Andrew Tombes, Henry Armetta.
JUDY'S SONGS
    Down on Melody Farm
    Swing, Mr, Mendelssohn, Swing
    Why? Because (with Fanny Brice)
    Swing Low, Sweet Chariot
    Bus Sequence

AMERICA'S GRANDEST FAMILY...IN THEIR NEWEST...
AND BEST...ADVENTURE!

HOWL! With Mickey Rooney...as he gets girls in his system...and finds he has no system with girls!

SWING! As Judy Garland sings swell new songs by Gordon & Revel!

SEE! Judge Hardy meet a dangerous crisis with the aid of a boy who thought he hated him!

Three's a crowd...but not for amorous Andy!

Remember "A Family Affair", "You're Only Young Once", "Judge Hardy's Children"? Judge Hardy's family is here again ... *grander than ever!*

Love FINDS
ANDY HARDY

The New Story of Judge Hardy's Family . . . with
LEWIS STONE · MICKEY ROONEY
JUDY GARLAND · CECILIA PARKER
FAY HOLDEN
Screen Play by William Ludwig · Directed by George B. Seitz
A Metro-Goldwyn-Mayer Picture

Judy in "LOVE FINDS ANDY HARDY"

LOVE FINDS ANDY HARDY (1938) - MGM
    Produced by Lou Ostrow
    Directed by George B. Seitz
    Screenplay by William Ludwig from the Stories by
        Vivien R. Bretherton
    Based on Characters Created by Aurania Rouverol
    Musical Score by David Snell
    Vocal Arrangements by Roger Edens
    Songs by Mack Gordon, Harry Revel and Roger Edens
    Costumes by Jeanne
    Photography by Lester White
    Film Editing by Ben Lewis
    CAST
        Lewis Stone, Mickey Rooney, Judy Garland (as Betsy Booth), Cecilia Parker, Fay Holden, Ann
        Rutherford, Betty Ross Clark, Lana Turner, Marie Blake, Don Castle, Gene Reynolds, Mary
        Howard, George Breakston, Raymond Hatton, Frank Darien, Rand Brooks, Erville Alderson.
    JUDY'S SONGS
        Meet the Beat of My Heart   *In Between*
        It Never Rains, But it Pours   *Bei Mir Bist Du Schoen* (cut before release)

Judy with Ray Bolger (as the Scarecrow) and
Jack Haley (as the Tin Woodsman)

THE WIZARD OF OZ (1939) - MGM Technicolor
Produced by Mervyn LeRoy
Directed by Victor Fleming
Screenplay by Noel Langley, Florence Ryerson & Edgar Allan Woolf
Adapted from the Book by L. Frank Baum
Color by Technicolor, opening and closing scenes in Sepia
Music Score by Herbert Stothart (and Roger Edens)
Songs by Harold Arlen and E.Y. Harburg
Musical Numbers Staged by Bobby Connolly
Art Direction by Cedric Gibbons and William A. Horning
Sets by Edwin B. Willis
Special Effects by Arnold Gillespie
Associate Conductor, George Stoll
Orchestral and Vocal Arrangements by George Bassman, Murray Cutter,
    Paul Marquardt, Ken Darby and Roger Edens
Character Make-up by Jack Dawn
Photography by Harold Rosson
Film Editing by Blanche Sewell
CAST
    Judy Garland (as Dorothy Gale), Frank Morgan, Ray Bolger, Bert Lahr, Jack Haley, Billie Burke,
    Margaret Hamilton, Charley Grapewin, Clara Blandick, Pat Walshe, Jerry Maren, Toto, The
    Singer Midgets.

JUDY'S SONGS
    Over the Rainbow
    Follow the Yellow Brick Road
    We're Off to See the Wizard
    Munchkinland
    The Jitterbug; Laugh a Day Away (cut before release)

Jack Haley, Ray Bolger, *Judy* and Bert Lahr in "THE WIZARD OF OZ"

Judy (as Dorothy)

Ray Bolger, Toto, *Judy* and Jack Haley in "THE WIZARD OF OZ"

Over the Rainbow

Lyric by E.Y. HARBURG
Music by HAROLD ARLEN

Lead - ing from your win - dow pane. To a place be - hind the

sun, Just a step be - yond the rain. _____

Chorus:

Some - where O - ver The Rain - bow way up high,

There's a land that I heard of once in a lul - la - by,

We're Off to See the Wizard

Lyric by E.Y. HARBURG
Music by HAROLD ARLEN

28

Fol-low the rain-bow o-ver the stream, Fol-low the fel-low who fol-lows a dream,

Fol-low, fol-low, fol-low, fol-low, Fol-low the yel-low brick road. We're

Chorus:

Off To See The Wiz-ard,_____ The won-der-ful Wiz-ard of Oz._____ We

hear he is a Whiz of a Wiz if ev-er a Wiz there was._____ If

ev-er, oh ev-er a Wiz there was, The Wiz-ard of Oz is one be-coz, be-

29

31

Charles D. Brown, unidentified player, Mickey Rooney
and *Judy* in "BABES IN ARMS"

Mickey Rooney and *Judy* in
"BABES IN ARMS"

BABES IN ARMS (1939) - MGM
Produced by Arthur Freed
Directed by Busby Berkeley
Screenplay by Jack McGowan and Kay Van Riper
Bassed on the Broadway Musical by Richard Rodgers and Lorenz Hart
Music and Lyrics by Richard Rodgers and Lorenz Hart
Musical Direction by George Stoll
Other Songs by Arthur Freed, Nacio Herb Brown, Gus Arnheim,
    Abe Lyman, E.Y. Harburg and Harold Arlen.
Orchestration by Conrad Salinger
Musical Adaption by Roger Edens
Costumes by Dolly Tree
Art Direction by Cedric Gibbons
Photography by Ray June
Film Editing by Frank Sullivan.
CAST
    Mickey Rooney, Judy Garland (as Patsy Barton), Charles Winninger, Guy Kibbee, June Preisser,
    Grace Hayes, Betty Jaynes, Douglas McPhail, Rand Brooks, Leni Lynn, John Sheffield, Henry
    Hull, Barnett Parker, Ann Shoemaker, Margaret Hamilton, Joseph Crehan, George McKay,
    Lelah Tyler, Lon McCallister.
JUDY'S SONGS
    I Cried for You   *Figaro*
    Good Morning   *Broadway Rhythm*
    Where or When   *Minstrel Show*
    God's Country   *Oh, Susanna*
    Babes in Arms   *I'm Just Wild About Harry*
    I Like Opera; I Like Swing   *My Day*

I'm Just Wild About Harry

Words and Music by NOBLE SISSLE and EUBIE BLAKE

Verse:

There's just one fel - low for me in this world,___ Har - ry's his name,___

That's what I claim,___ Why for ev - 'ry fel - low there

must be a girl,___ I've found my mate,___ be kind-ness of fate.___

Chorus:

I'm Just Wild ___ A - bout Har - ry, ___ And Har - ry's wild

___ a - bout me, ___ The heav'n - ly bliss - es

of his kiss - es Fill me with ec - sta - sy, ___

___ He's sweet, just like ___ choc-'late can - dy, ___ And

34

I Cried for You

Words and Music by ARTHUR FREED,
GUS ARNHEIM and ABE LYMAN

Mickey Rooney and *Judy* in "ANDY HARDY MEETS DEBUTANTE"

ANDY HARDY MEETS DEBUTANTE (1940) - MGM
Produced by J.J. Cohn
Directed by George B. Seitz
Screenplay by Annalee Whitmore and Thomas Seller
Based on Characters Created by Aurania Rouverol
Songs; *"Alone"* by Arthur Freed and Nacio Herb Brown
        "I'm Nobody's Baby" by Lester Santley, Benny Davis
        and Milton Ager
Musical Score by David Snell
Musical Arrangements by George Stoll
Musical Arrangements by Roger Edens
Musical Conductor, George Stoll
Photography by Sidney Wager, and Charles Lawton, Jr.
Costumes by Dolly Tree
Film Editing by Harold F. Kress
CAST
        Lewis Stone, Mickey Rooney, Judy Garland (as Betsy Booth), Cecilia Parker, Fay Holden, Ann
        Rutherford, Diana Lewis, Sara Haden, George Breakston, George Lessey, Harry Tyler, Gladys
        Blake, Addison Richards, Cy Kendall.
JUDY'S SONGS
        Alone   *All I Do is Dream of You*
        I'm Nobody's Baby   *Buds Won't Bud* (cut before release)

Mickey Rooney and *Judy* in "STRIKE UP THE BAND"

STRIKE UP THE BAND (1940) - MGM
  Produced by Arthur Freed
  Directed by Busby Berkeley
  Screenplay by John Monks, Jr. and Fred Finklehoffe
  Music and Lyrics by Roger Edens and Arthur Freed, George
      and Ira Gershwin
  Chorals and Orchestrations by Conrad Salinger and Leo Arnaud
  Musical Direction by George Stoll
  Photography by Ray June
  Film Editing by Ben Lewis
CAST
    Mickey Rooney, Judy Garland (as Mary Holden), June Preisser, William Tracy, Larry Nunn,
    Margaret Early, Enid Bennett, Ann Shoemaker, Sarah Edwards, Milton Kibbee, Virginia Brissac,
    Helen Jerome Eddy, Francis Pierlot, Paul Whiteman and his Orchestra.
JUDY'S SONGS
    Nobody   *Strike Up the Band*
    Drummer Boy   *My Wonderful One, Let's Dance*
    Do the La Conga   *The Dear Gay Nineties*
    Nell of New Rochelle   *Heaven Will Protect the Working Girl*
    Our Love Affair

Our Love Affair

Words and Music by ARTHUR FREED and ROGER EDENS

George Murphy, *Judy,* Charles Winninge , Arthur Shields and passengers in "LITTLE NELLIE KELLY"

LITTLE NELLIE KELLY (1940) - MGM

Produced by Arthur Freed
Directed by Norman Taurog
Screenplay by Jack McGowan
Based on the Musical Comedy by George M. Cohan
Song, *"Singin' in the Rain"* by Arthur Freed and Nacio Herb Brown
Musical Adaptation by Roger Edens
Musical Direction by George Stoll
Costumes by Dolly Tree
Photography by Ray June
Film Editing by Frederick Y. Smith

CAST

Judy Garland (as Nellie Kelly and her mother), George Murphy, Charles Winninger, Douglas MacPhail, Arthur Shields, James Burke, Robert Homans, Thomas Dillon, Rita Page, Henry Blair, Forrester Harvey, Frederick Worlock.

JUDY'S SONGS

A Pretty Girl Milking Her Cow
It's a Great Day for the Irish
Singin' in the Rain
Danny Boy (cut before release)

It's a Great Day for the Irish

Words and Music by ROGER EDENS

Moderately—March tempo

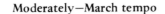

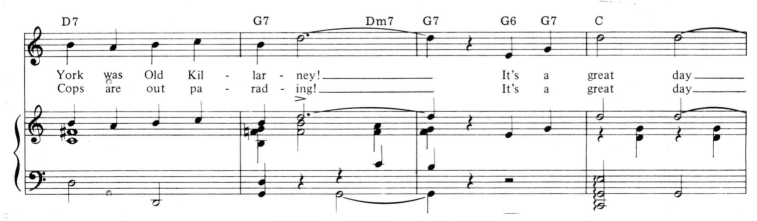

44

Lewis Stone, *Judy* and Mickey Rooney in "LIFE BEGINS FOR ANDY HARDY"

LIFE BEGINS FOR ANDY HARDY (1941) - MGM
    Produced by J.J. Cohn
    Directed by George B. Seitz
    Screenplay by Agnes Christine Johnston
    Based on Characters Created by Aurania Rouverol
    Musical Direction by George Stoll
    Costumes by Kalloch
    Art Direction by Cedric Gibbons
    Photography by Lester White
    Film Editing by Elmo Vernon
CAST
    Lewis Stone, Mickey Rooney, Judy Garland (as Betsy Booth), Fay Holden, Ann Rutherford, Sara
    Haden, Patricia Dane, Ray McDonald, George Breakston, Pierre Watkin.
JUDY'S SONGS (All were cut before release)
    Easy to Love   *Abide With Me*
    The Rosary   *America*

Jackie Cooper and *Judy* in "ZIEGFELD GIRL"

ZIEGFELD GIRL (1941) - MGM
      Produced by Pandro S. Berman
      Directed by Robert Z. Leonard
      Screenplay by Marguerite Roberts and Sonya Levien
      Original Story by William Anthony Mcguire
      Musical Numbers Directed by Busby Berkeley
      Musical Direction by George Stoll
      Orchestration and Vocals by Leo Arnaud, George Bassman
          and Conrad Salinger
      Music and Lyrics by Nacio Herb Brown, Gus Kahn, Roger Edens, Ralph Freed,
          Harry Carroll, Joseph McCarthy, Edward Gallagher,
          Al Shean, John Schonberger, Richard Coburn, Vincent
          Rose, Harold Adamson and Walter Donaldson
      Costumes by Adrian
      Make-up by Jack Dawn
      Art Direction by Cedric Gibbons
      Sets by Edwin B. Willis
      Sound by Douglas Shearer
      Photography by Ray June
      Film Editing by Blanche Sewell
      CAST
          James Stewart, Judy Garland (as Susan Gallagher), Hedy Lamarr, Lana Turner, Jackie Cooper,
          Tony Martin, Ian Hunter, Charles Winninger, Edward Everett Horton, Philip Dorn, Paul Kelly, Eve
          Arden, Dan Dailey, Jr., Mae Busch, Al Shean, Fay Holden, Rose Hobart, Felix Bressart, Bernard
          Nedell, Renie Riano, Josephine Whittell, Jean Wallace, Myrna Dell, Georgia Carroll, Leslie
          Brooks, Claire James, Louise LaPlanche, Frances Gladwin, Patricia Dane, Anya Taranda.
      JUDY'S SONGS
          Minnie from Trinidad   *Laugh? I Thought I'd Split My Sides*
          I'm Always Chasing Rainbows   *We Must Have Music* (cut before release)

I'm Always Chasing Rainbows

Words by JOSEPH McCARTHY
Music by HARRY CARROLL

rain, Some fel - lows make a win - ning some - time, I

nev - er e - ven make a - gain. Be - lieve me, I'm Al - ways Chas - ing

Rain - bows, Wait - ing to find a lit - tle blue - bird in

vain. _____ vain. _____

49

BABES ON BROADWAY (1941) - MGM

Produced by Arthur Freed
Directed by Busby Berkeley
Screenplay by Fred Finklehoffe and Elaine Ryan
Musical Adaptation by Roger Edens
Songs by E.Y. Harburg, Burton Lane, Ralph Freed,
    Roger Edens, Harold Rome
Musical Direction by George Stoll
Vocals and Orchestrations by Leo Arnaud, George Bassman and
    Conrad Salinger
Costumes by Kalloch
Photography by Lester White
Film Editing by Frederick Y. Smith

CAST

Mickey Rooney, Judy Garland (as Penny Morris), Fay Bainter, Virginia Weidler, Ray McDonald, Richard Quine, Donald Meek, James Gleason, Emma Dunn, Frederick Burton, Cliff Clark, Alexander Woollcott, William Post, Jr., Donna Reed, Luis Alberni, Joe Yule.

JUDY'S SONGS

Babes on Broadway   *Hoe Down*
I'm a Yankee Doodle Dandy   *Chin Up! Cheerio! Carry On!*
How About You   *Minstrel Show*
Mary is a Grand Old Name   *Franklin D. Roosevelt Jones*
I've Got Rings on My Fingers   *Waiting for the Robert E. Lee*
Bombshell from Brazil   *Blackout Over Broadway*

Ray McDonald, Richard Quine, Virginia Weidler, Fay Bainter and *Judy* in "BABES ON BROADWAY"

Judy, Joe Yule, Jr. (Mickey Rooney's father) and James Gleason in "BABES ON BROADWAY"

Street Scene: "BABES ON BROADWAY"

How About You?

Words by RALPH FREED
Music by BURTON LANE

George Murphy, *Judy* and Gene Kelly in "FOR ME AND MY GAL"

Judy, Gene Kelly and stagehand in "FOR ME AND MY GAL"

FOR ME AND MY GAL (1942) · MGM

Produced by Arthur Freed
Directed by Busby Berkeley
Screenplay by Richard Sherman, Fred Finklehoffe and Sid Silvers
Original Story by Howard Emmett Rogers
Musical Adaptation by Roger Edens
Dance Direction by Bobby Connolly
Vocals and Orchestration by Conrad Salinger,
  George Bassman and Leo Arnaud
Costumes by Kalloch
Photographed by William Daniels
Film Editing by Ben Lewis

CAST

 Judy Garland (as Jo Hayden), George Murphy, Gene Kelly, Marta Eggerth, Ben Blue, Richard Quine,
 Keenan Wynn, Horace McNally, Lucille Norman.

JUDY'S SONGS

After You've Gone	*Don't Leave Me, Daddy*
How Ya Gonna Keep 'Em Down on the Farm	*It's A Long Way To Tipperary*
Ballin The Jack	*Smiles*
For Me and My Gal	*Pack Up Your Troubles*
When You Wore A Tulip	*Goodbye Broadway, Hello France*
Where Do We Go From Here	*Til We Meet Again*

For Me and My Gal

Words by EDGAR LESLIE and E. RAY GOETZ
Music by GEORGE W. MEYER

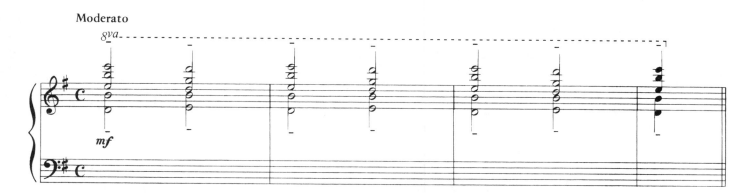

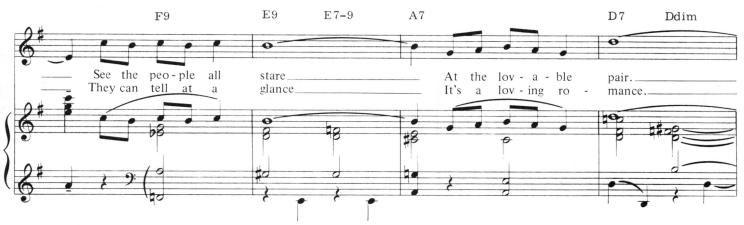

In his wed-ding ar - ray_____ Hear him smil - ing - ly say:_____
Gee! it makes the boy proud_____ As he says to the crowd:_____

Chorus:

"The bells are ring - ing_____ For Me And My Gal,_____

The birds are sing - ing_____ For Me And My Gal._____

Ev - 'ry - bod-y's been know - ing_____ To a wed-ding they're go - ing_____

And for weeks they've been sew - ing,_____ Ev - 'ry Su - sie and Sal._____

After You've Gone

By CREAMER and LAYTON

now don't for-get it, There'll come a time,— when you'll re-gret it;
we've been to-geth-er, Their joys and tears,— all kinds of weath-er;

Some day, when you grow lone-ly, Your heart will break like mine and
Some day, blue and down-heart-ed, You'll long to be with me right

you'll want me on-ly, Af-ter You've Gone,— Af-ter You've Gone a-
back where you start-ed; Af-ter I'm gone,— Af-ter I'm gone a-

way._____
way._____

Van Heflin and *Judy* in "PRESENTING LILY MARS"

PRESENTING LILY MARS (1943) - MGM
   Produced by Joseph Pasternak
   Directed by Norman Taurog
   Screenplay by Richard Connell and Gladys Lehman
   Based on the novel by Booth Tarkington
   Songs by Walter Jurmann, Paul Francis Webster, Merrill Pye,
      E.Y. Harburg, Burton Lane, Roger Edens
   Musical Direction by George Stoll
   Musical Adaptation by Roger Edens
   Dance Direction by Ernst Matray
   Gowns by Howard Shoup
   Photographed by Joseph Ruttenberg
   Film Editing by Albert Akst
CAST
   Judy Garland (as Lily Mars), Van Heflin, Fay Bainter, Richard Carlson, Spring Byington, Connie
   Gilchrist, Marta Eggerth, Ray McDonald, Leonid Kinskey, Annabelle Logan, Janet Chapman, Patricia
   Barker, Douglas Croft, Marilyn Maxwell, Tommy Dorsey and his orchestra, Bob Crosby and his
   orchestra, Charles Walters.
JUDY'S SONGS
   When I Look At You
   Tom, Tom, The Piper's Son
   Every Little Movement
   Broadway Rhythm
   Paging Mr. Greenback (cut before release)

Every Little Movement
(Has a Meaning All Its Own)

Words by OTTO HARBACH
Music by KARL HOSCHNA

las was false._____
soul in - flame._____

The schot - tische and the
Your arms and legs the grow

pol - ka swing, She's laid____ them all a - way._____ Aes -
el - o - quent And in - ner thoughts sub - lime_____ Ex -

thet - ic danc - ing is____ the thing That holds the "floor" to -
press____ them - selves with temp - 'ra - ment While you are keep - ing

day._____ Ah!
time._____ Ah!

Moderato grazioso

Chorus:

Ev - 'ry Lit - tle Move - ment has a mean - ing all its own,

Ev - 'ry thought and feel - ing by some pos - ture can be shown, _____ And ev - 'ry

love - thought_ that comes a - steal - ing o'er your be - ing _ must be re - veal - ing All its

sweet - ness_ in some ap - peal - ing lit - tle ges - ture_ all, all its own.   own.

rall.

a tempo

Broadway Rhythm

Words by ARTHUR FREED
Music by NACIO HERB BROWN

me, Ev - 'ry - bod - y sing and dance! _____

Oh _____ that Broad - way Rhy - thm _____

Oh, _____

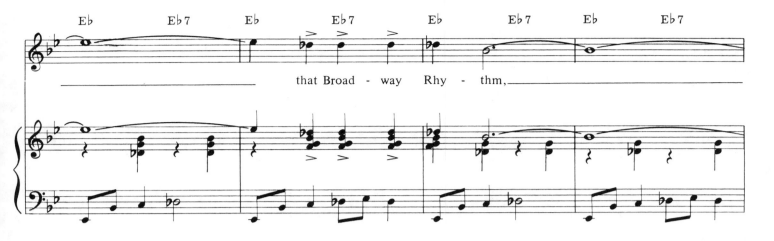

that Broad - way Rhy - thm,_____

When I hear that hap - py beat___

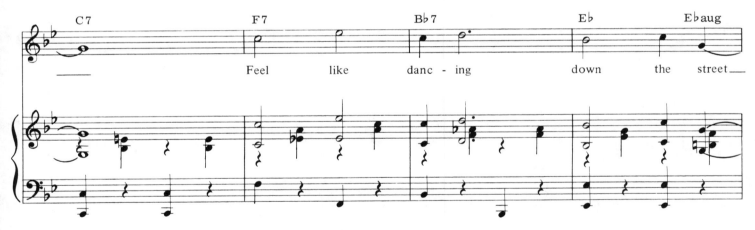

Feel like danc - ing down the street___

To _____ that Broad - way

Rhy - thm writh - ing beat - ing rhy - thm.

Got - ta dance! Got - ta dance! Got - ta

dance! Got - ta dance! Broad - way___ Rhy - thm___

___ It's got ___ me, Ev - 'ry - bod - y dance! _____

THOUSANDS CHEER (1943) - MGM Technicolor
    Produced by Joseph Pasternak
    Directed by George Sidney
    Screenplay by Paul Jarrico and Richard Collins
    Based on their story "Private Miss Jones"
    Musical Adaptation by Herbert Stothart
    Costumes by Irene
    Photographed by George Folsey
    Film Editing by George Boemler
CAST
    Kathryn Grayson, Gene Kelly, Mary Astor, Jose Iturbi, John Boles, Ben Blue, Dick Simmons, Frances Rafferty, Odette Myrtil, Mary Elliott, Frank Jenks, Wally Cassell, Frank Sully, Betty Jaynes.
GUEST STARS
    Mickey Rooney, Judy Garland, Red Skelton, Eleanor Powell, Ann Sothern, Lucille Ball, Lena Horne, Virginia O'Brien, Marsha Hunt, Marilyn Maxwell, Frank Morgan, Donna Reed, June Allyson, Margaret O'Brien, Gloria DeHaven, Lionel Barrymore, John Conte, Sara Haden, Connie Gilchrist, Marta Linden, Kay Kyser and his Orchestra, Bob Crosby and his Orchestra, Benny Carter and his Band, Don Loper and Maxine Barrat.
JUDY'S SONGS
    The Joint is Really Jumping by Ralph Blane and Hugh Martin

Judy with Mickey Rooney in "GIRL CRAZY"

GIRL CRAZY (1943) - MGM
>   Produced by Arthur Freed
>   Directed by Norman Taurog
>   Screenplay by Fred Finklehoffe
>   Original story by Guy Bolton and Jack McGowan
>   Music and Lyrics by George and Ira Gershwin
>   Musical Adaptation by Roger Edens
>   Musical Direction by George Stoll
>   Costumes by Irene
>   Orchestrations by Conrad Salinger, Axel Stordahl and Sy Oliver
>   Dance Direction by Charles Walters
>   Photographed by William Daniels and Robert Planck
>   Film Editing by Albert Akst
>   CAST
>   Mickey Rooney, Judy Garland (as Ginger Gray), Gil Stratton, Nancy Walker, June Allyson, Robert E.
>   Strickland, Rags Ragland, Guy Kibbee, Frances Rafferty, Howard Freeman, Henry O'Neill, Sidney
>   Miller, Sarah Edwards, William Bishop, Eve Whitney, Barbara Bedford, Hazel Brooks, Peter Lawford,
>   Don Taylor, Bess Flowers, Georgia Carroll, Tommy Dorsey and his Orchestra.
>   JUDY'S SONGS
>   *But Not for Me*   *Bidin' My Time*
>   *Embraceable You*   *I Got Rhythm*
>   *Could You Use Me*

Embraceable You

Music and Lyrics by GEORGE GERSHWIN and IRA GERSHWIN

Bidin' My Time

Music and Lyrics by GEORGE GERSHWIN and IRA GERSHWIN

I Got Rhythm

Music and Lyrics by GEORGE GERSHWIN and IRA GERSHWIN

Lively, with abandon

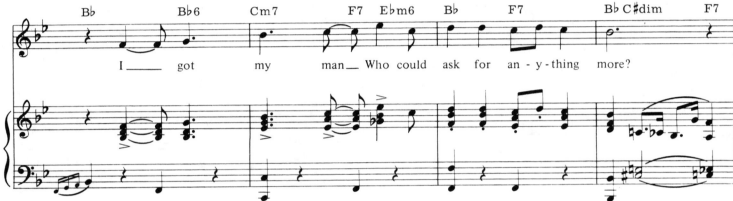

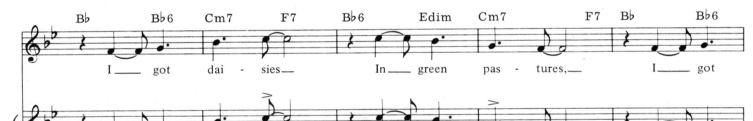

Trou - ble,_ I_ don't mind him,_ You_ won't find him_ 'Round_my door. I_ got star - light,_ I_ got sweet dreams,_ I_ got my man _ Who could ask for an - y - thing

more, Who could ask for an - y - thing more? more?

But Not for Me

Music and Lyrics by GEORGE GERSHWIN and IRA GERSHWIN

Judy and Tom Drake in "MEET ME IN ST. LOUIS"

On the "MEET ME IN ST. LOUIS" set: Left to right, Lucille Bremer, Mary Astor, Joan Carroll, Harry Davenport, *Judy*, Margaret O'Brien and Henry Daniels, Jr.

MEET ME IN ST. LOUIS (1944) - MGM Technicolor
Produced by Arthur Freed
Directed by Vincente Minnelli
Screenplay by Irving Brecher and Fred Finklehoffe
Based on Book by Sally Benson
Musical Adaptation by Roger Edens
Musical Direction by George Stoll
Orchestration by Conrad Salinger
Dance Direction by Charles Walters
Photography by George Folsey
Costumes by Sharaff
Film Editing by Albert Akst
New Songs by Hugh Martin and Ralph Blane
CAST
   Judy Garland (as Esther Smith), Margaret O'Brien, Mary Astor, Lucille Bremer, Tom Drake, Marjorie
   Main, Leon Ames, Harry Davenport, Joan Carroll, June Lockhart, Henry Daniels, Jr., Hugh Marlowe,
   Robert Sully, Chill Wills, Darryl Hickman, Donald Curtis, Mary Jo Ellis, Belle Mitchell, Victor Kilian.
JUDY'S SONGS
   The Boy Next Door   *Skip to My Lou*
   Have Yourself a Merry Little Xmas   *Under the Bamboo Tree*
   The Trolley Song   *Over the Bannister*
   Meet Me in St. Louis, Louis   *Boys and Girls Like You and Me* (cut before release)

The Trolley Song

Music by RALPH BLANE
Lyric by HUGH MARTIN

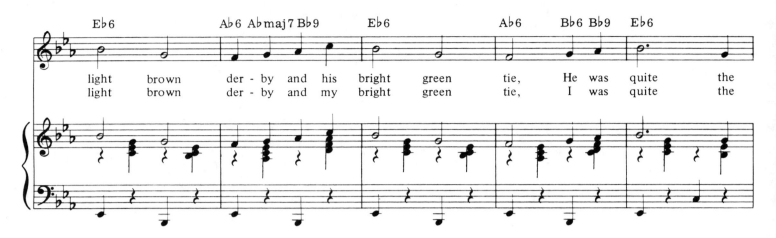

light brown der - by and his bright green tie, He was quite the
light brown der - by and my bright green tie, I was quite the

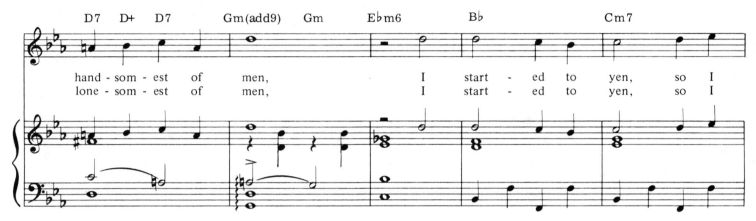

hand - som - est of men, I start - ed to yen, so I
lone - som - est of men, I start - ed to yen, so I

count - ed to ten, then I count - ed to ten a - gain. _____
count - ed to ten, then I count - ed to ten a - gain. _____

gliss. on white keys

Meet Me in St. Louis, Louis

Words by ANDREW B. STERLING
Music by KERRY MILLS

dance the Hooch - ee Kooch - ee, _____ I will be your toot - sie woot - sie; _____ Meet Me In St. Lou - is, Lou - is, Meet me

at the fair." _____ fair." _____

The Boy Next Door

Words and Music by HUGH MARTIN and RALPH BLANE

The mo-ment I saw him smile, I knew he was
The mo-ment I saw her smile, I knew she was

just my style, My on-ly re-gret is
just my style, My on-ly re-gret is

we've nev-er met, For I dream of him all the while.
we've nev-er met, For I dream of her all the while.

94

Have Yourself a Merry Little Christmas

Words and Music by RALPH BLANE and HUGH MARTIN

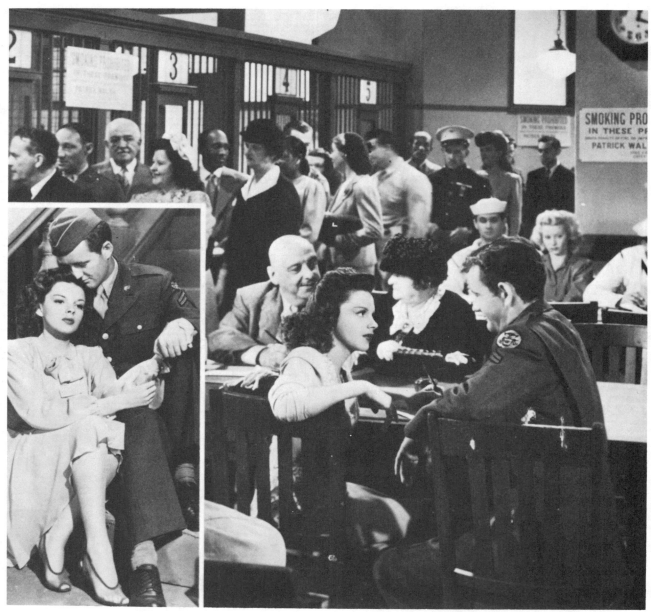

Judy with Robert Walker in "THE CLOCK"

THE CLOCK (1945) - MGM
> Produced by Arthur Freed
> Directed by Vincente Minnelli
> Screenplay by Robert Nathan and Joseph Schrank
> From Original Story by Paul and Pauline Jarrico
> Musical Score by George Bassman
> Costumes by Irene and Marion Herwood Keyes
> Special Effects by A. Arnold Gillespie
> Photography by George Folsey
> Film Editing by George White
> CAST
>> Judy Garland (as Alice Mayberry), Robert Walker, James Gleason, Keenan Wynn, Marshall Thompson, Lucile Gleason, Moyna MacGill, Ruth Brady, Chester Clute, Dick Elliott, Arthur Space, Ray Teal.

Judy in "The Interview" sequence in "ZIEGFELD FOLLIES OF 1946"

ZIEGFELD FOLLIES (1946) - MGM Technicolor
    Produced by Arthur Freed
    Directed by Vincente Minnelli
    Songs by Harry Warren, Arthur Freed, George and Ira Gershwin,
        Ralph Blane, Hugh Martin, Earl Brent, Ralph Freed, Roger
        Edens, Philio Brahva, and Douglas Furber, Kay Thompson.
    Musical Direction by Lennie Hayton
    Orchestrations by Kay Thompson
    Photography by George Folsey, Charles Rocher and Ray June
    Costumes by Irene, designed by Irene Sharaff and Helen Rose
    Dance Direction by Robert Alton
    Film Editing by Albert Akst

CAST
    Fred Astaire, Lucille Ball, Lucille Bremer, Fanny Brice, Judy Garland, Kathryn Grayson, Lena Horne,
    Gene Kelly, James Melton, Victor Moore, Red Skelton, Esther Williams, William Powell, Cyd
    Charisse, Marion Bell, Edward Arnold, Ray Teal, Naomi Childers, Hume Cronyn, William Frawley,
    Robert Lewis, Harriet Lee, Rex Evans, Bunin Puppets

JUDY'S SONG
    A Great Lady has an Interview, written by Roger Edens and Kay Thompson, staged by Charles
    Walters and directed by Vincente Minnelli.

John Hodiak and *Judy*

Judy sings "On The Atchison, Topeka and The Santa Fe"

Judy on set

THE HARVEY GIRLS (1946) - MGM

Produced by Arthur Freed
Directed by George Sidney
Screenplay by Edmund Beloin and Nathaniel Curtis
Additional Dialogue by Kay Van Riper
Based on the Book by Samuel Hopkins Adams
Songs by Johnny Mercer and Harry Warren
Orchestrations by Conrad Salinger
Musical Direction by Lennie Hayton
Vocal Arrangements by Kay Thompson
Musical Numbers Staged by Robert Alton
Photography by George Folsey
Film Editing by Albert Akst

CAST

Judy Garland (as Susan Bradley), John Hodiak, Ray Bolger, Angela Lansbury, Preston Foster, Virginia O'Brien, Marjorie Main, Kenny Baker, Cyd Charisse, Selena Royle, Catherine McLeod, Chill Wills, Ruth Brady, Jack Lambert, Horace McNally, Ben Carter, Ray Teal, Hazel Brooks, Bunny Waters, Peggy Maley, Jacqueline White, Eve Whitney.

JUDY'S SONGS

On the Atchison, Topeka and the Santa Fe
In the Valley Where the Evening Sun Goes Down
It's a Great Big World
Swing Your Partner Round and Round

Hayride (cut before release)
March of the Doagies (cut before release)
My Intuition (cut before release)

On the Atchison, Topeka and the Santa Fe

Words by JOHNNY MERCER
Music by HARRY WARREN

Moderately *(with rhythm)*

Do yuh hear that whis-tle down the line?___ I fig-ure that it's en-gine num-ber

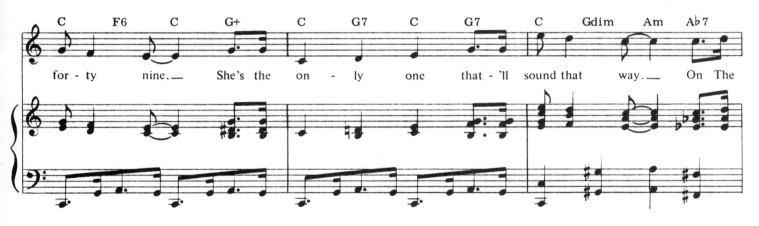

for-ty nine,___ She's the on-ly one that-'ll sound that way.___ On The

Atch-i-son, To-pe-ka And The San-ta Fe.___ See the

Judy with Fred Astaire in "EASTER PARADE"

EASTER PARADE (1948) - MGM Techicolor
    Produced by Arthur Freed
    Associate Producer, Roger Edens
    Directed by Charles Walters
    Screenplay by Sidney Sheldon, Frances Goodrich and Albert Hackett
    Original Story by Frances Goodrich and Albert Hackett
    Songs by Irving Berlin
    Musical Direction by Johnny Green
    Orchestrations by Conrad Salinger, Mason Van Cleave and Leo Arnaud
    Vocal Arrangements by Robert Tucker
    Costumes by Irene
    Photographed by Harry Stradling
    Musical Numbers staged and directed by Robert Alton
    Film Editing by Albert Akst
CAST
    Judy Garland (as Hannah Brown), Fred Astaire, Peter Lawford, Ann Miller, Clinton Sundberg, Jules Munshin, Jeni LeGon, Jimmy Bates, Richard Beavers, Dick Simmons, Dee Turnell, Lola Albright, Joi Lansing.

JUDY'S SONGS
Better Luck Next Time	*Ragtime Violin*
Michigan	*Snookey Ookums*
It Only Happens When I Dance With You	*A Couple of Swells*
A Fella With An Umbrella	*Easter Parade*
I Love A Piano	*Mr. Monotony* (cut before release)
When That Midnight Choo Choo Leaves For Alabam	

Judy sings "Who" with the chorus in "TILL THE CLOUDS ROLL BY"

TILL THE CLOUDS ROLL BY (1946) - MGM Technicolor
Produced by Arthur Freed
Directed by Richard Whorf
Screenplay by Myles Connolly and Jean Holloway
Story by Guy Bolton, adapted by George Wells
Based on the life and music of Jerome Kern
Musical Direction by Lennie Hayton
Orchestrations by Conrad Salinger
Vocal Arrangements by Kay Thompson
Musical Numbers staged and directed by Robert Alton
Photographed by Harry Stradling and George Folsey
Costumes supervised by Irene; designed by Helen Rose
Film Editing by Albert Akst
CAST
    Robert Walker, Judy Garland (as Marilyn Miller), Lucille Bremer, Van Heflin, Dorothy Patrick, Mary Nash, Paul Langton, Joan Wells, Harry Hayden and William "Bill" Phillips, with June Allyson, Kathryn Grayson, Lena Horne, Van Johnson, Angela Lansbury, Gower Champion, Cyd Charisse, Tony Martin, Ray McDonald, Virginia O'Brien, Dinah Shore, Frank Sinatra, Caleb Peterson, and The Wilde Twins.
JUDY'S SONGS
    Who? (directed by Vincente Minnelli)
    Look For The Silver Lining (directed by Vincente Minnelli)
    D'ye Love Me? (cut before release)

Who?

Lyrics by OTTO HARBACH and OSCAR HAMMERSTEIN II
Music by JEROME KERN

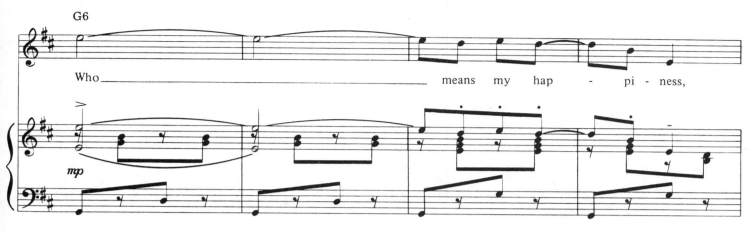

Who_____ means my hap - pi - ness,

Who_____ would I an - swer: yes,

to?_____ { Well, you ought_____ to guess
Darned if I_____ can guess

1.   2.

who,_____ no one but you._____
who,_____ no one but you._____

Look for the Silver Lining

Words by BUDDY DeSYLVA
Music by JEROME KERN

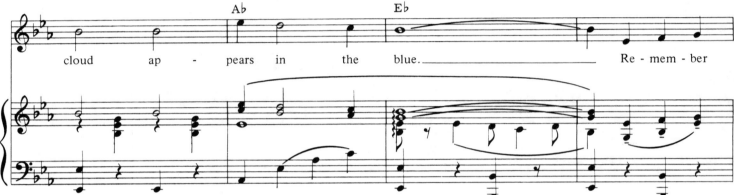

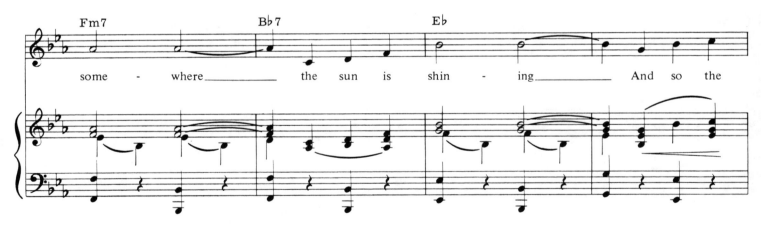

shine for you. A heart, full _____ of joy and
glad - ness _____ Will al - ways ban - ish sad - ness and
strife _____ So al - ways Look For _____ The Sil - ver
Lin - ing _____ And try to find the sun - ny side of

life.

life. _____

Judy with Gene Kelly in "THE PIRATE"

THE PIRATE (1948), MGM Technicolor
    Produced by Arthur Freed
    Direced by Vincente Minnelli
    Screenplay by Albert Hackett and Frances Goodrich
    From the play by S.N. Behrman
    Songs by Cole Porter
    Musical Direction by Lennie Hayton
    Instrumental arrangements by Conrad Salinger
    Vocal arrangements by Kay Thompson, Robert Tucker and Roger Edens
    Dance direction by Robert Alton and Gene Kelly
    Photographed by Harry Stradling
    Costumes supervised by Irene; designed by Tom Keogh
    Film Editing by Blanche Sewell
    CAST
        Judy Garland (as Manuela), Gene Kelly, Walter Slezak, Gladys Cooper, Reginald Owen, George Zucco, The Nicholas Brothers, Lester Allen, Lola Deem, Ellen Ross, Mary Jo Ellis, Jean Dean, Marion Murray.
    JUDY'S SONGS
        You Can Do No Wrong   *Be A Clown*
        Mack The Black   *Voodoo* (cut before release)
        Love Of My Life

Be a Clown

Words and Music by COLE PORTER

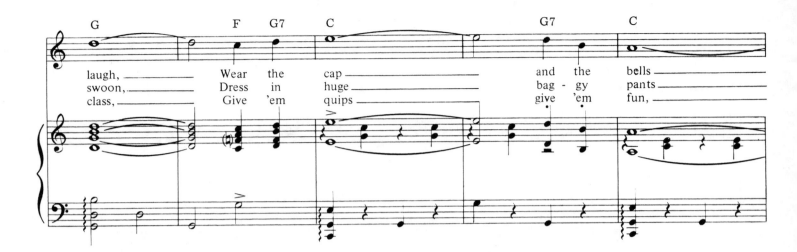

laugh, _____ Wear the cap _____ and the bells _____
swoon, _____ Dress in huge _____ bag - gy pants _____
class, _____ Give 'em quips _____ give 'em fun, _____

_____ And you'll rate with all _____ the great swells, _____ If
_____ And you'll ride the road _____ to ro - mance, _____ A
_____ And they'll pay to say _____ you're A - 1, _____ If

you be - come a doc - tor, folks - 'll face you with dread, _____ If you be - come a
butch - er or a bak - er la - dies nev - er em - brace, _____ A bar - ber for a
you be - come a farm - er you've the weath - er to buck, _____ If you be - come a

den - tist, they'll be glad when you're dead,_____ You'll get a big - ger
beau would be a so - cial dis - grace,_____ They all - 'll come to
gam - bler, you'll be stuck with your luck_____ But jack you'll nev - er

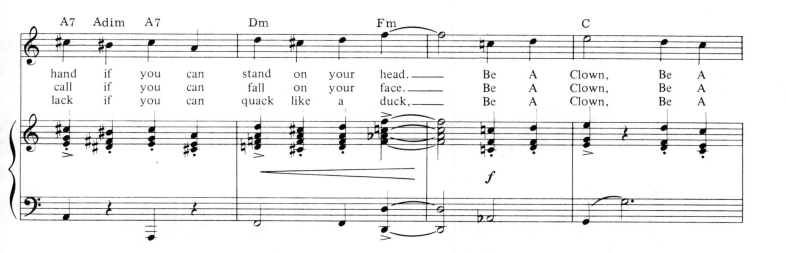

hand if you can stand on your head._____ Be A Clown, Be A
call if you can fall on your face._____ Be A Clown, Be A
lack if you can quack like a duck,_____ Be A Clown, Be A

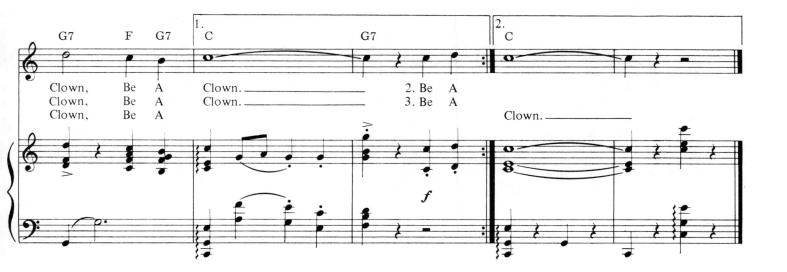

Clown, Be A Clown._____ 2. Be A
Clown, Be A Clown._____ 3. Be A
Clown, Be A   Clown._____

Judy with Arthur Freed, Nacio Herb Brown and piano player

WORDS AND MUSIC (1948) - MGM Technicolor
Produced by Arthur Freed
Directed by Norman Taurog
Screenplay by Fred Finklehoffe
Story by Guy Bolton and Jean Holloway
Adaptation by Ben Feiner, Jr.
Songs by Richard Rodgers and Lorenz Hart
Musical Direction by Lennie Hayton
Orchestrations by Conrad Salinger
Vocal Arrangements by Robert Tucker
Musical Numbers staged and choreographed by Robert Alton
Photographed by Charles Rosher and Harry Stradling
Costumes by Helen Rose
Film Editing by Albert Akst and Ferris Webster
CAST
   Perry Como, Mickey Rooney, Ann Sothern, Tom Drake, Betty Garrett, Janet Leigh, Marshall Thompson, Jeanette Nolan, Richard Quine, Clinton Sundberg, Cyd Charisse, Harry Antrim, Ilka Gruning.
GUEST STARS
   Judy Garland, June Allyson, Lena Horne, Gene Kelly, Vera Ellen, The Blackburn Twins, Allyn Ann McLerie, John Butler, Dee Turnell, Mel Torme.
JUDY'S SONGS
   Johnny One Note
   I Wish I Were In Love Again

I Wish I Were in Love Again

Words by LORENZ HART
Music by RICHARD RODGERS

sleep all night,___ Ap - pe - tite and health re - stored.

You don't know how much I'm bored!

Chorus:

1. The sleep - less nights, The dai - ly fights, The quick to - bog - gan when you
2. (The) fur - tive sigh, The black - ened eye, The words "I'll love you till the

reach the heights; I miss the kiss - es and I miss the bites, I
day I die," The self de - cep - tion that be - lieves the lie. I

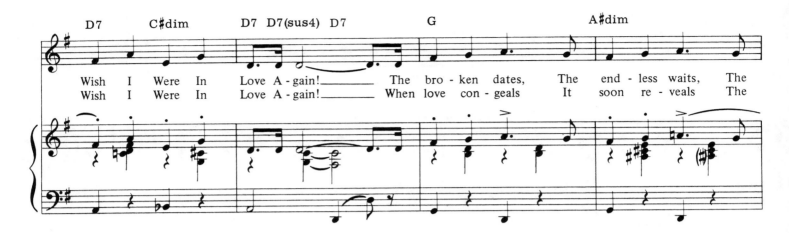

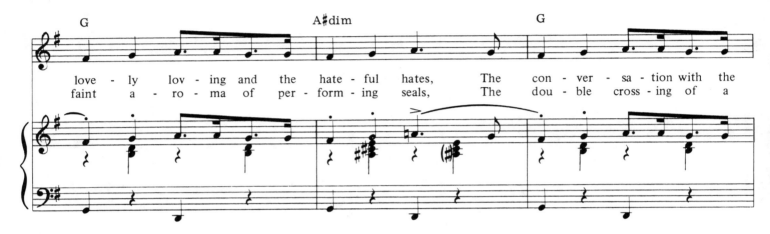

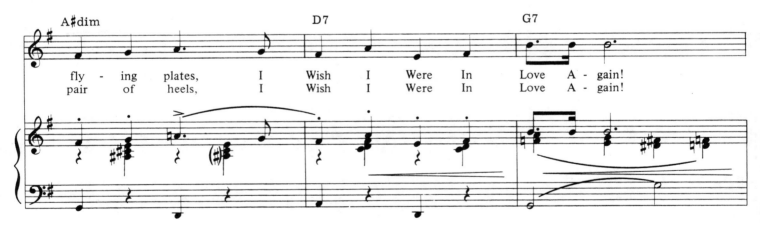

119

Johnny One Note

Words by LORENZ HART
Music by RICHARD RODGERS

Brightly

Poor John - ny One - Note__ Sang out__ with gus - to__ And

just o - ver - lord - ed__ the place._____

Poor John - ny One - Note__ Yelled wil - ly - nil - ly,__ Un -

til he__ was blue in__ the face,_____ For

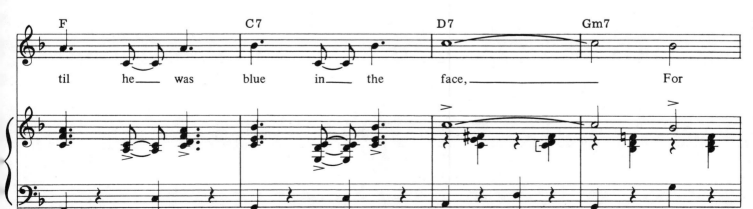

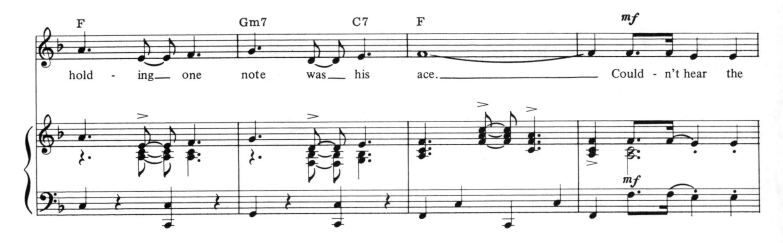

hold - ing— one note was— his ace.———————— Could - n't hear the

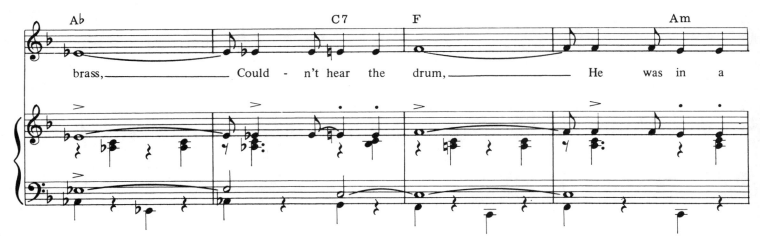

brass,———————— Could - n't hear the drum,———————— He was in a

class———————— By him - self, by gum!————————

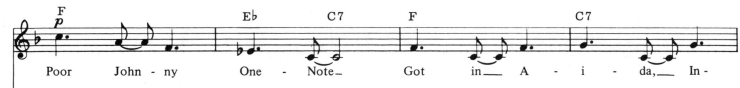

Poor John - ny One - Note— Got in— A - i - da, In-

deed a ___ great chance to ___ be brave._____

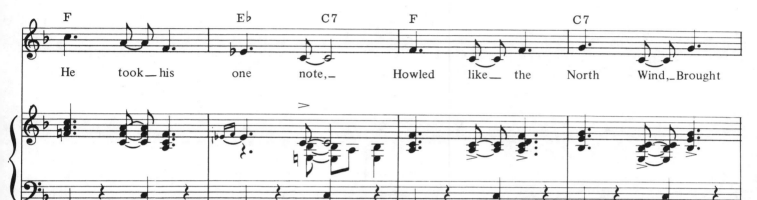

He took ___ his one note, ___ Howled like ___ the North Wind, Brought

forth wind ___ that made crit - ics rave, _____ While

Ver - di turned 'round in ___ his grave! _____ Could - n't hear the

Chorus:

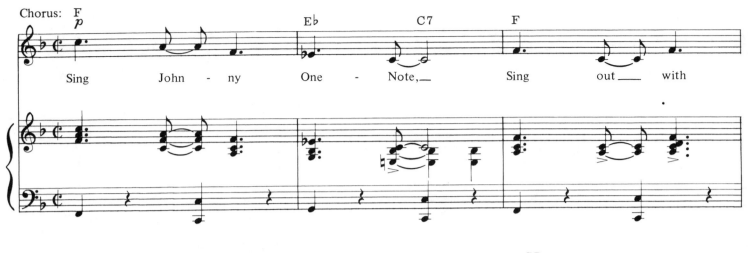

Sing Johnny One-Note,— Sing out with

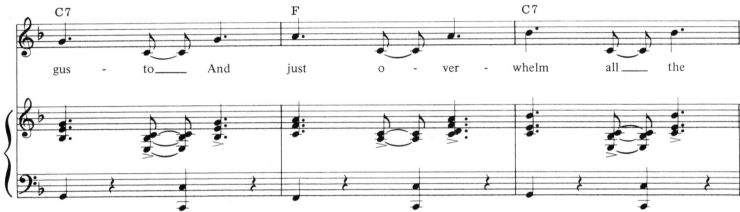

gus-to— And just o-ver-whelm all— the

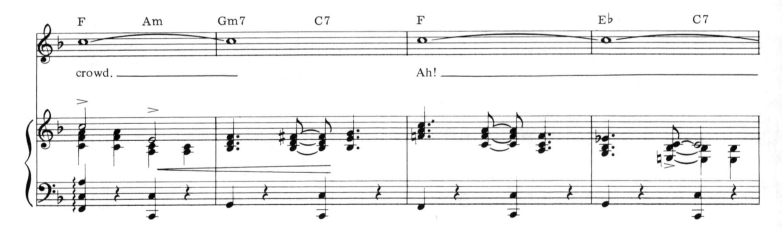

crowd._____ Ah! _____

So sing, John - ny One - Note,— out

loud!_____ Sing, John - ny One - Note!_____

Sing John - ny

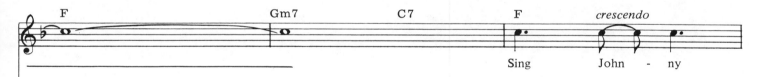
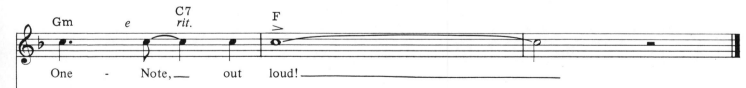

One - Note,_ out loud!_____

Van Johnson, *Judy* and S.Z. "Cuddles" Sakall in "IN THE GOOD OLD SUMMERTIME"

IN THE GOOD OLD SUMMERTIME (1949) - MGM Technicolor
Produced by Joseph Pasternak
Directed by Robert Z. Leonard
Screenplay by Albert Hackett, Frances Goodrich and Ivan Tors
Based on a scenario by Samson Raphaelson
From the play, "The Shop Around The Corner" by Miklos Laszlo
Musical Numbers directed by Robert Alton
Music direction by George Stoll
Photographed by Harry Stradling
Film Editing by Adrienne Fazan

CAST
    Judy Garland (as Veronica Fisher), Van Johnson, S.Z. Sakall, Spring Byington, Buster Keaton, Marcia
    Van Dyke, Clinton Sundberg, Lillian Randolph, Ralph Sanford, Liza Minnelli.

JUDY'S SONGS
    I Don't Care   *Meet Me Tonight In Dreamland*
    Merry Christmas   *In The Good Old Summertime*
    Play That Barbershop Chord   *Last Night When We Were Young* (cut before release)
    Put Your Arms Around Me, Honey

Last Night When We Were Young

Lyric by E.Y. HARBURG
Music by HAROLD ARLEN

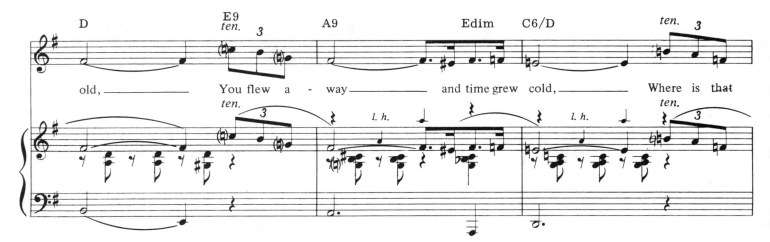

old, _____ You flew a - way _____ and time grew cold, _____ Where is that

star _____ that seemed so bright, _____ A - ges a - go last

night? To think _____ that spring had de - pend - ed _____ on mere - ly

this _____ a look, a kiss, To think _____ that some-thing so

splen - did _____ could slip a - way _____ In one lit - tle day - break, *l. h.* So

now _____ let's rem - i - nisce _____ and rec - ol -

lect _____ the sighs and the kiss - es, _____ The arms that

clung _____ when we were young last night. _____

1.   2. G

_____   Last _____

I Don't Care

Words by JEAN LENOX
Music by HARRY O. SUTTON

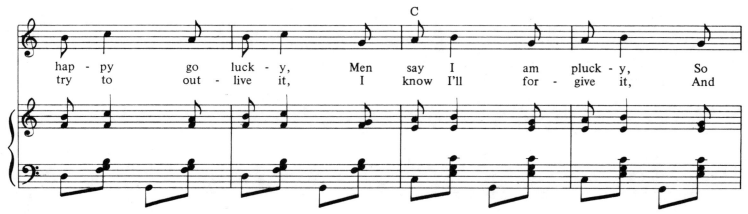

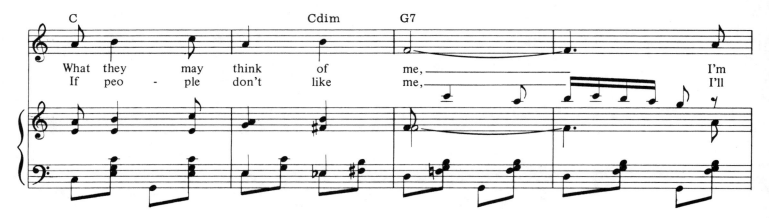

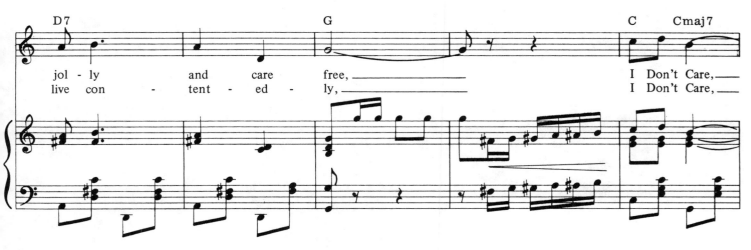

jol - ly   and   care   free, _____   I Don't Care, _____
live   con - tent - ed - ly, _____   I Don't Care, _____

_____ I Don't Care, _____   If I   do   get the mean and
_____ I Don't Care, _____   If peo - ple   do not try to

Slow

sto - ny stare,   If I'm nev - er suc - cess - ful, It won't be   dis - tress - ful, 'Cos
treat me fair,   There is naught can a - maze me, Dis - like can   not daze me, 'Cos

I   Don't   Care.
I   Don't   Care. _____

Gene Kelly, *Judy* and Phil Silvers in "SUMMER STOCK"

Judy sings "Get Happy" in "SUMMER STOCK"

Judy with Gene Kelly in "SUMMER STOCK"

Judy singing "Get Happy" in "SUMMER STOCK"

SUMMER STOCK (1950) - MGM Technicolor
    Produced by Joseph Pasternak
    Directed by Charles Walters
    Screenplay by George Wells and Sy Gomberg
    Musical Direction by Johnny Green and Saul Chaplin
    Orchestrations by Conrad Salinger and Skip Martin
    Dances staged by Nick Castle
    Photographed by Robert Planck
    Costumes by Walter Plunkett
    Film Editing by Albert Akst
    CAST
        Judy Garland (as Jane Falbury), Gene Kelly, Eddie Bracken, Gloria DeHaven, Marjorie Main, Phil Silvers, Carleton Carpenter, Ray Collins, Nita Bieber, Hans Conried.
    JUDY'S SONGS
        Get Happy
        Friendly Star
        Happy Harvest
        If You Feel Like Singing
        You Wonderful You

Get Happy

Lyric by TED KOEHLER
Music by HAROLD ARLEN

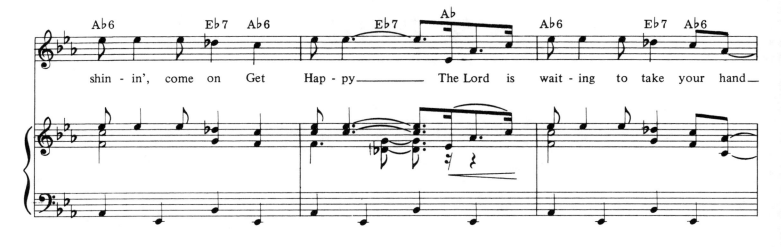

shin - in', come on Get Hap - py_____ The Lord is wait - ing to take your hand_

_____ Shout Hal - le - lu - jah! come on, Get Hap - py_____ We're go -

ing to the prom - ised land. We're head - in'_____ 'cross the

Riv - er,_____ wash your sins 'way_____ in the tide. It's

James Mason, *Judy* and Charles Bickford in
"A STAR IS BORN"

Judy with James Mason in "A STAR IS BORN"

A STAR IS BORN (1954), A Warner Bros. Release, A Transcona Enterprises Prod.

Produced by Sidney Luft
Associate Producer, Vern Alves
Directed by George Cukor
Screenplay by Moss Hart
Based on a screenplay by Dorothy Parker, Alan Campbell and
      Robert Carson
Story by William A. Wellman and Robert Carson
Songs by Harold Arlen and Ira Gershwin
"Born in a Trunk" number by Leonard Gershe
Musical Direction by Ray Heindorf
Dances by Richard Barstow
Costumes by Irene Sharaff and Jean Louis
Vocal Arrangemens by Jack Cathcart
Orchestrations by Skip Martin
Photographed by Sam Leavitt
Film Editing by Folmer Blangsted

CAST

    Judy Garland (as Esther Blodgett (Vicki Lester)), James Mason, Jack Carson, Charles Bickford,
    Tommy Noonan, Lucy Marlowe, Amanda Blake, Irving Bacon, Percy Helton, Joan Shawlee, Hazel
    Shermet, Lotus Robb, Nancy Kulp, Louis JeanHeydt, Grady Sutton, Richard Webb.

JUDY'S SONGS

The Man That Got Away	*I'll Get By*
Gotta Have Me Go With You	*You Took Advantage Of Me*
It's A New World	*The Peanut Vendor*
Someone At Last	*Swanee*
Born In A Trunk	*Here's What I'm Here For* (cut before release)
My Melancholy Baby	*Lose That Long Face* (cut before release)

The Man that Got Away

Lyric by IRA GERSHWIN
Music by HAROLD ARLEN

Swanee

Words by IRVING CAESAR
Music by GEORGE GERSHWIN

Verse:

I've been a-way from you a long time

I nev-er thought I'd miss you so

Some-how I feel

Your love was real,

Near you I long to

be,_____ The birds are sing - ing, It is

song time,_____ The ban - jos strum - min' soft and low,_____

I know that you Yearn for me too;

Swan - ee You're call - ing me.

Chorus:

Swan - ee How I love you, How I love you My

145

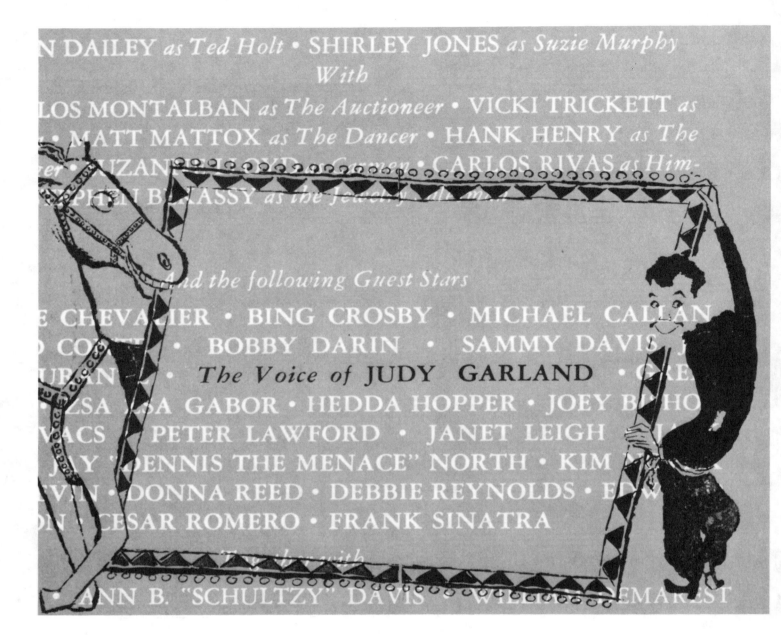

N DAILEY *as Ted Holt* • SHIRLEY JONES *as Suzie Murphy*
With

LOS MONTALBAN *as The Auctioneer* • VICKI TRICKETT *as*
MATT MATTOX *as The Dancer* • HANK HENRY *as The*
CARLOS RIVAS *as Him-*

And the following Guest Stars

E CHEVALIER • BING CROSBY • MICHAEL CALLAN
BOBBY DARIN • SAMMY DAVIS
The Voice of JUDY GARLAND
SA GABOR • HEDDA HOPPER • JOEY BISHO
PETER LAWFORD • JANET LEIGH
DENNIS THE MENACE" NORTH • KIM
DONNA REED • DEBBIE REYNOLDS •
CESAR ROMERO • FRANK SINATRA

ANN B. "SCHULTZY" DAVIS

PEPE (1960) - Columbia (CinemaScope and Eastman Color)
  Produced and Directed by George Sidney
  Associate Poducer, Jacques Gelman
  Screenplay by Dorothy Kingsley and Claude Binyon
  Based on a play by L. Bush-Fekete
  Story by Leonard Spigelgass and Sonya Levien
  Music Supervision and backround score by Johnny Green
  Choreography by Eugene Loring and Alex Romero
  Gowns by Edith Head
  Photography by Joe MacDonald
  Film Editing by Viola Lawrence and Al Clark
CAST
  Cantinflas, Dan Dailey, Shirley Jones, Carlos Montalban, Ernie Kovacs, Jay North, Vicki Trickett, Matt Mattox, William Demarest, Michael Callan, Hank Henry, Suzanne Lloyd, Lela Bliss, Ray Walker.
GUEST STARS
  Maurice Chevalier, Bing Crosby, Richard Conte, Bobby Darin, Sammy Davis Jr., Jimmy Durante, Zsa Zsa Gabor, Greer Garson, Hedda Hopper, Joey Bishop, Peter Lawford, Janet Leigh, Jack Lemmon, Kim Novak, Donna Reed, Debbie Reynolds, Edward G. Robinson, Cesar Romero, Frank Sinatra, Ann B. Davis, Billie Burke, Dean Martin, Charles Coburn, Tony Curtis, Carlos Rivas, and The Voice of Judy Garland.
JUDY'S SONGS
  The Faraway Part of Town, by Andre Previn and Dory Langdon, was nominated for an Academy Award. Shirley Jones and Dan Dailey danced to the song sung by Judy on the soundtrack.

Judy (as Irene Hoffman) in "JUDGMENT AT
NUREMBERG"

JUDGMENT AT NUREMBERG (1961) - United Artists
    Produced by Stanley Kramer
    Associate Producer, Phillip Langner
    Screenplay by Abby Mann, based on his television script
    Production designed by Rudolph Sternad
    Music by Ernest Gold
    Photographed by Ernest Laszlo
    Costumes by Joe King
    Film Editing by Fred Knudston
    CAST
        Spencer Tracy, Burt Lancaster, Richard Widmark, Marlene Dietrich, Maximilian Schell, Judy Garland
        (as Irene Hoffman), Montgomery Clift, William Shatner, Edward Binns, Virginia Christine, Alan
        Baxter, Kenneth MacKenna, Werner Klemperer, Sheila Bromley, Karl Swenson, Ray Teal, Martin
        Brandt, Olga Fabian, John Wengraf, Howard Caine

Judy and Bruce Ritchey in "A CHILD IS WAITING"

Judy (as Jean Hansen) in "A CHILD IS WAITING"

A CHILD IS WAITING (1962) - A United Artist Release, A Stanley Kramer Production
Produced by Stanley Kramer
Associate Producer, Phillip Langner
Directed by John Cassavetes
Screenplay by Abby Mann, based on his television play.
Music by Ernest Gold
Photographed by Joseph LaShelle
Film Editing by Gene Fowler Jr.
CAST
    Burt Lancaster, Judy Garland (as Jean Hansen), Gena Rowlands, Steven Hill, Bruce Ritchey, Gloria McGehee, Paul Stewart, Elizabeth Wilson, Barbara Pepper, June Walker, Lawrence Tierney.

GAY PURR-EE (1962) - A Warner Bros. Release, A UPA Production
Executive Poducer, Henry G. Saperstein
Associate Poducer, Lee Orgel
Directed by Abe Leviton
Screenplay by Dorothy and Chuck Jones
Music by Harold Arlen and E.Y. Harburg
Music Arranged and Conducted by Mort Lindsey
Vocal Arrangements by Joseph J. Lilley
Photography by Roy Hutchcroft, Dan Miller, Jack Stevens and
      Duane Keegan
Art Direction by Victor Haboush
Film Editing by Ted Baker

A full-length animated feature, with the voices of:
Judy Garland (as Mewsette), Robert Goulet, Hermione Gingold, Red Buttons, Morey Amsterdam,
Paul Frees, Mel Blanc, Julie Bennett, Joan Gardner.
JUDY'S SONGS
      Paris Is A Lonely Town
      Take My Hand, Paree
      Roses Red, Violets Blue
      Little Drops Of Rain
      The Mewsette Finale

Judy (who supplied the voice for Mewsette) in "GAY PURR-EE"

Paris Is a Lonely Town

Lyric by E.Y. HARBURG
Music by HAROLD ARLEN

chim - ney's moan, the riv - er cries, each glam - or - ous bridge is a bridge of sighs;

Riv - er, riv - er, won't you be my lov - er? Don't _____ turn me

down For Par - is is such a lone - ly, lone - ly

town.

Judy and Dirk Bogarde in "I COULD GO ON SINGING"

I COULD GO ON SINGING (1963) - United Artist, A Barbican Production, Panavision - Eastman Color
Produced by Stuart Millar and Lawrence Turman
Directed by Ronald Neame
Screenplay by Mayo Simon
Story by Robert Dozier
Musical Supervision by Saul Chaplin
Music by Mort Lindsey
Costumes by Edith Head
Photography by Arthur Ibbetson
New Songs by Harold Arlen and E.Y. Harburg
Film Editing by John Shirley
CAST
    Judy Garland (as Jenny Bowman), Dirk Bogarde, Jack Klugman, Gregory Phillips, Aline MacMahon, Pauline Jameson, Jeremy Brunham, Russell Waters, Gerald Sim, Leon Cortez.
JUDY'S SONGS
    I Could Go On Singing
    Hello Bluebird
    It Never Was You
    By Myself
    I Am The Monarch Of The Sea

Hello Blue Bird

Words and Music by CLIFF FRIEND

By Myself

Words by HOWARD DIETZ
Music by ARTHUR SCHWARTZ

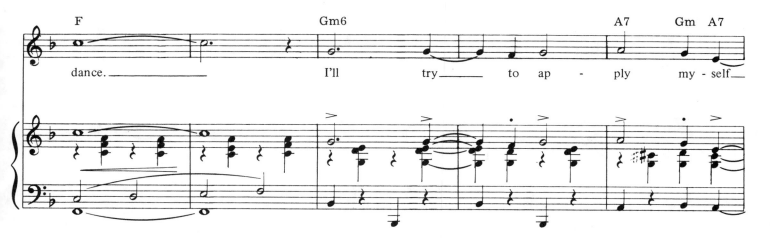

dance._____ I'll try_____ to ap - ply my - self____

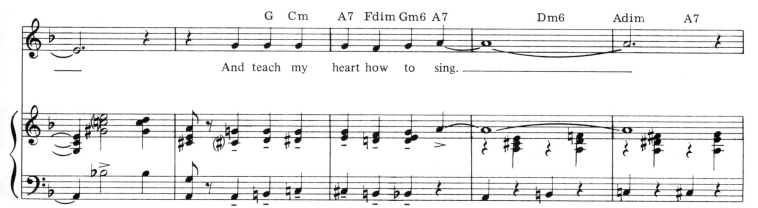

____ And teach my heart how to sing._____

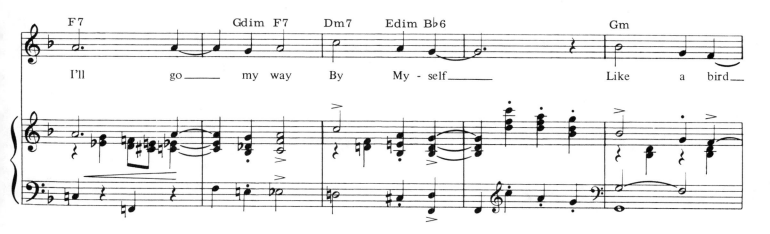

I'll go_____ my way By My - self_____ Like a bird____

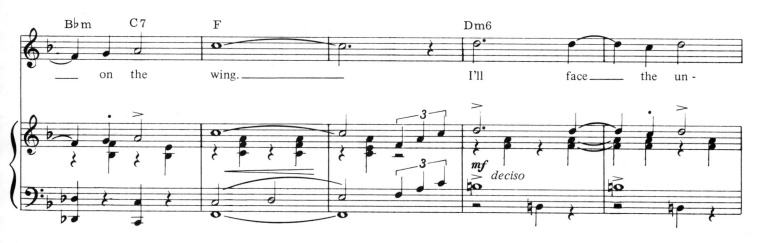

____ on the wing._____ I'll face_____ the un -

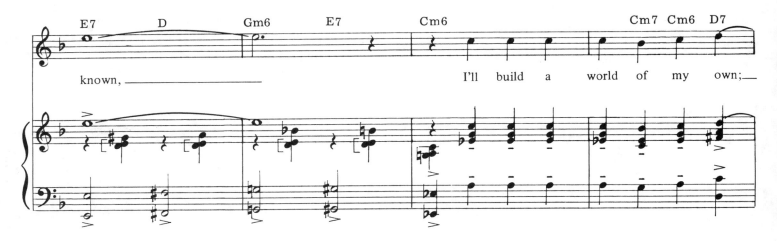

known, _____

I'll build a world of my own;

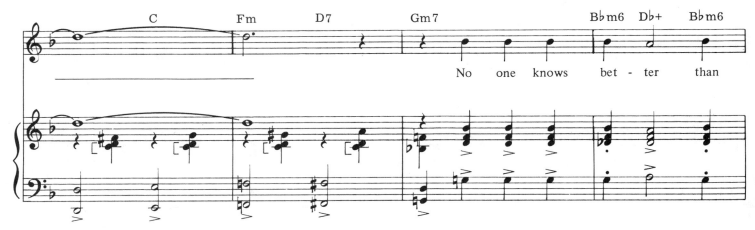

_____

No one knows bet - ter than

I my - self, _____ I'm By My - self _____ a-

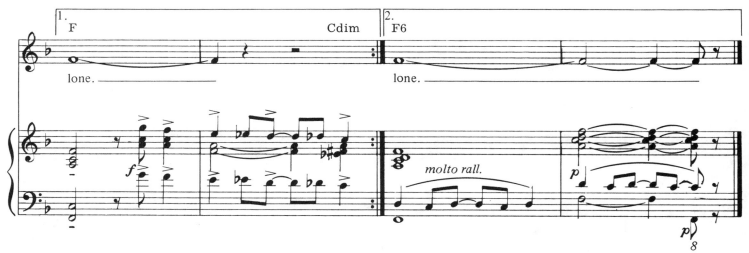

lone. _____

lone. _____

JUDY GARLAND: IN CONCERT

"---In an oblique and daffy sort of way, you are as much a national asset as our coal reserves - both of you help warm up our insides."
Your devoted fan, Billy Rose

JUDY GARLAND'S MOST FAMOUS CONCERTS

Philadelphia Orchestra	July 10, 1943
The Palladium, London	April 14, 1951
	June 25, 1951
The Palace, New York City	October 16, 1951
Los Angeles Philharmonic	April 26, 1952
The Curran, San Francisco	June 4, 1952
The Palladium,	November 18, 1954
The Palace,	September 26, 1956
The Metropolitian Opera House, New York City	May 11, 1959
The Palladium	August 28, 1960
	September 4, 1960
	December 1, 1960
Carnegie Hall, New York City	April 23, 1961
The Palladium	July 23, 1964
	November 8, 1964
	November 16, 1964
Westbury Music Fair, Long Island	July, 1967
The Palace	August 18, 1967
Garden State Arts Center, New Jersey	June 25, 1968

----And 100 more!

Ad for the "Metropolitan Opera House" performance

Ad for the "At Home at the Palace" performance

Liza Minnelli and *Judy* perform on "THE JUDY GARLAND SHOW" television series

Ray Bolger and Judy singing "A Couple of Swells"

Judy at the Palace, 1967

Judy at the Palace in 1951

Judy rehearses "Over The Rainbow" with pit musicians at Carnegie Hall in 1961

Almost Like Being in Love

Words by ALAN JAY LERNER
Music by FREDERICK LOEWE

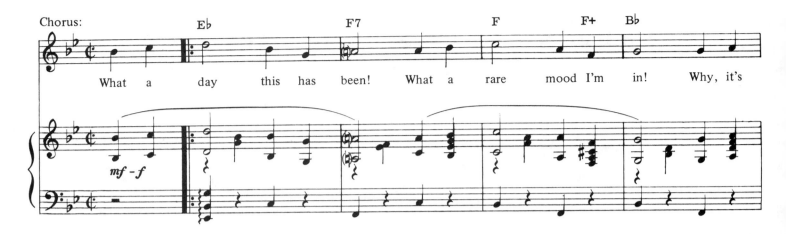

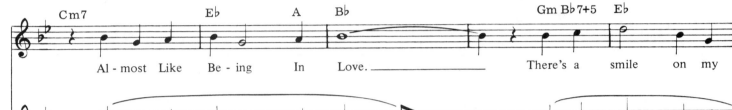

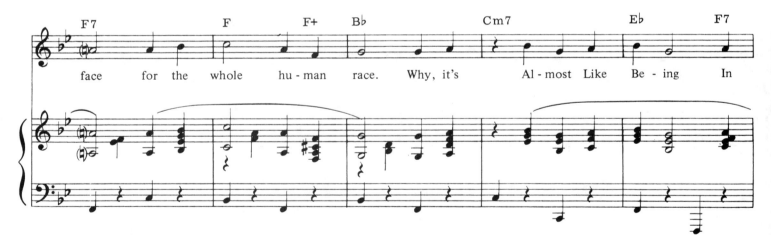

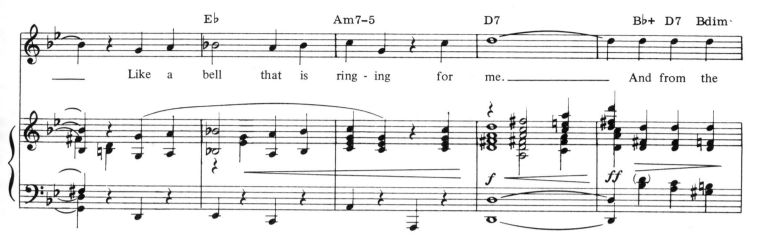

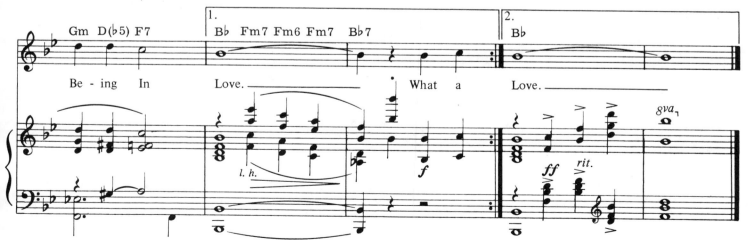

Alone Together

Words by HOWARD DIETZ
Music by ARTHUR SCHWARTZ

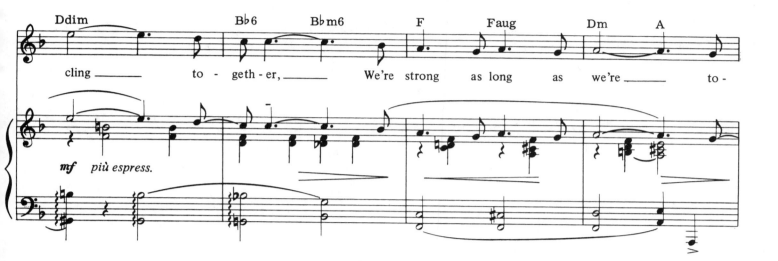

172

love _____ can be; _____ And we _____ can

weath-er_____ The great un - known,_____ If we're A -

lone _____ To - geth - er._____ A

geth - er, _____ to - geth-er._____

Am I Blue?

Words by GRANT CLARKE
Music by HARRY AKST

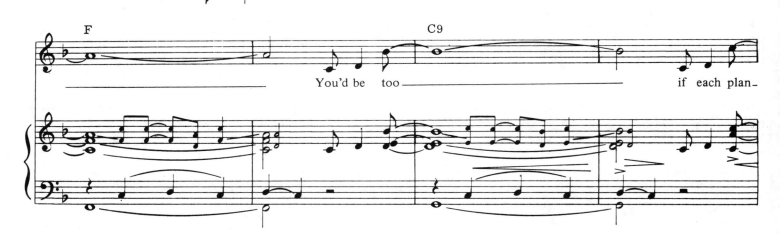

Any Place I Hang My Hat Is Home

Words by JOHNNY MERCER
Music by HAROLD ARLEN

Slowly, with a steady rock

Free___ an' eas-y that's my style___ How-dy do me

watch me smile,___ Fare___ thee well me af-ter-while___

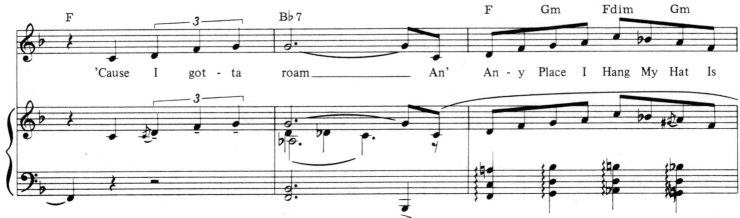

'Cause I got-ta roam_____ An' An-y Place I Hang My Hat Is

Home!

Sweet - nin' wa - ter

cher - ry wine,____ Thank____ you kind - ly, suits me fine____

Kan - sas Cit - y, Car - o - line,____ That's my hon - ey - comb,____

____'Cause An - y Place I Hang My Hat Is Home.

Birds roost-in' in the tree pick up an' go An' the go-in' proves That's how it ought to be, I pick up too When the spir-it moves me. Cross___ the riv-er round the bend,_ How - dy stran-ger so long friend,_ There's a

178

voice in the lone-some win' that keeps whis-per-in' roam!

I'm go-in' where a wel-come mat is, No mat-ter where that is 'Cause

An - y Place I Hang My Hat Is Home.

Home.

Come Rain or Come Shine

Words by JOHNNY MERCER
Music by HAROLD ARLEN

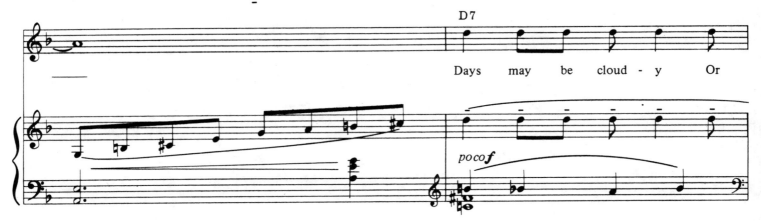

Do I Love You

Words and Music by COLE PORTER

Moderato, in steady rhythm, without dragging

Do I Love You, do I? Does-n't one and one make two? Do I Love You, do I? Does Ju-ly need a sky of blue?

From This Moment On

Words and Music by COLE PORTER

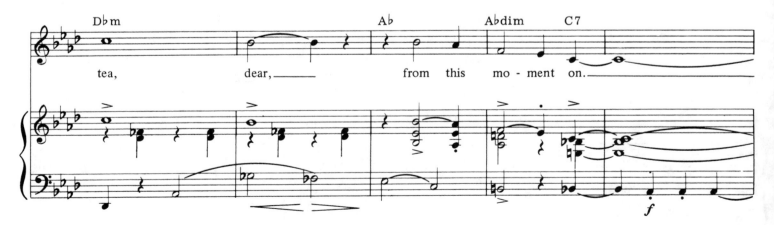

From this hap - py day, _____

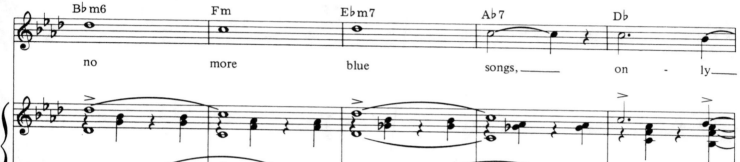

no   more   blue   songs, ____ on - ly ____

____ whoop - dee - doo   songs, ____   from this mo - ment on. ____

_____ For you've got the love ____ I

need so much, ___ Got the skin ___ I love to touch, ___

Got the arms ___ to hold me tight, ___

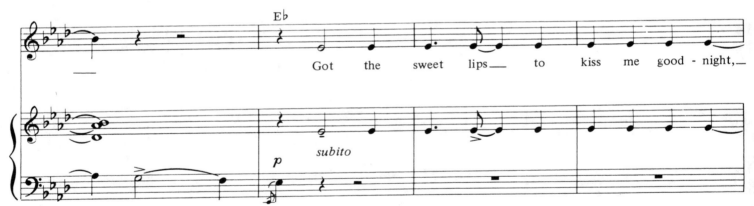

Got the sweet lips ___ to kiss me good - night, ___

From this mo - ment on, ___

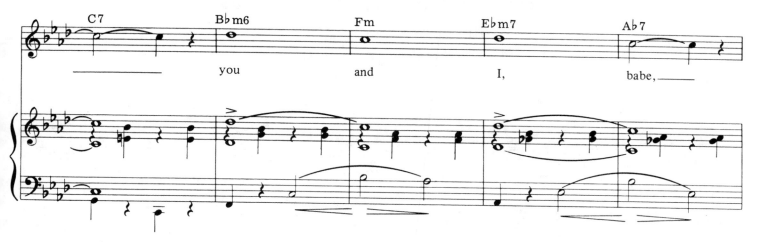

you   and   I,   babe,

we'll   be___   rid - in' high,   babe,___   Ev - 'ry

care   is   gone_____   from   this   mo - ment

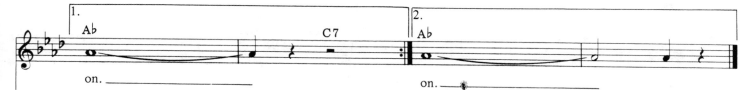

1.   2.

on. _____   on. _____

Blues in the Night

(My Mama Done Tol' Me)

Words by JOHNNY MERCER
Music by HAROLD ARLEN

ma - ma done tol' me,____) A whoo-ee - duh-whoo - ee,____ Ol'

click - e - ty clack's a - ech - o - in' back th' Blues____ In The Night,____ The eve-nin'

breeze - 'll start the trees to cry-in' and the moon - 'll hide its light,

when you get the Blues____ In The Night.____

194

I Feel a Song Comin' On

Words and Music by JIMMY McHUGH,
DOROTHY FIELDS and GEORGE OPPENHEIMER

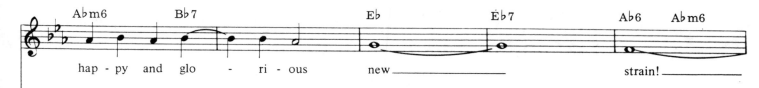

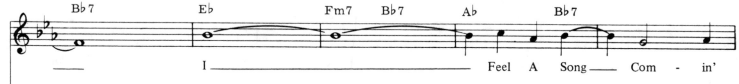

I Happen to Like New York

Words and Music by COLE PORTER

more I think of it. I like the sight and the sound and e-ven the stink of it, I

Hap-pen To Like New York. I like to go to Bat-ter-y Park And

watch those lin-ers boom-ing in. I of-ten ask my-self, why should it be_____ That

they should come so far from a-cross the sea,_____ I sup-pose it's be-cause they all a-

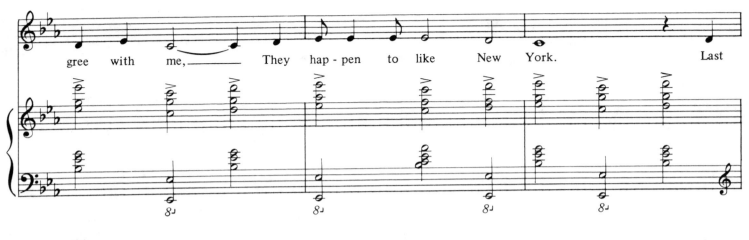

gree with me,_____ They hap-pen to like New York. Last

Sun-day af-ter-noon I took a trip to Hack-en-

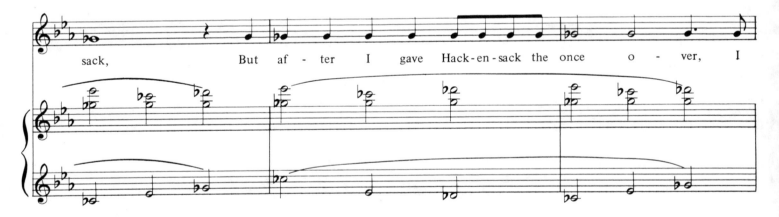

sack, But af-ter I gave Hack-en-sack the once o - ver, I

took the next train back. I Hap-pen To Like New York, I

hap - pen to love this burg And when I have to give the world a

last fare - well, And the un - der - tak - er starts to ring my fun -'ral bell, I don't

want to go to heav - en, don't want to go to h... I Hap - pen To Like New

York, I Hap - pen To Like _____ New York. _____

If Love Were All

Words and Music by NOEL COWARD

more you give your trust, The more you're bound to lose: Al - though _____

_____ when shad - ows fall _____ I think if on - ly

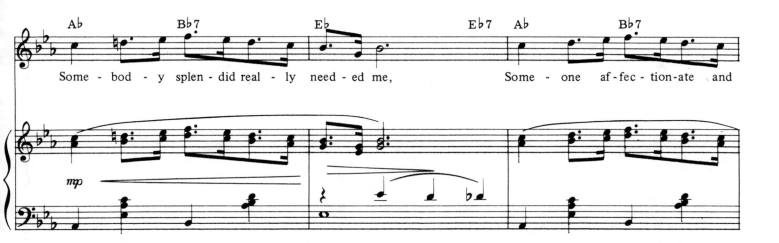

Some - bod - y splen - did real - ly need - ed me, Some - one af - fec - tion - ate and

Make Someone Happy

Words by BETTY COMDEN and ADOLPH GREEN
Music by JULE STYNE

lights when it nears you, One {man girl} you're ev - 'ry - thing to. Fame, _____ if you win it, Comes and goes _____ in a min - ute. Where's the real _____ stuff in life to cling to? Love _____ is the an - swer, Some - one to

Just in Time

Words by BETTY COMDEN and ADOLPH GREEN
Music by JULE STYNE

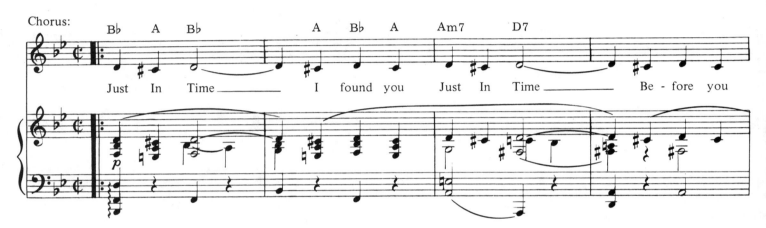

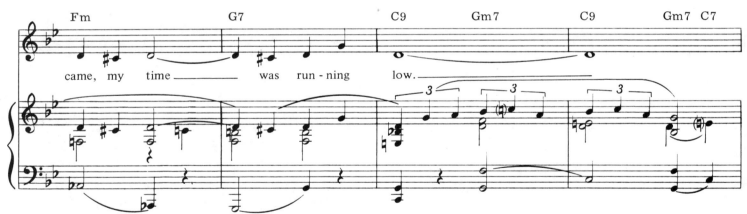

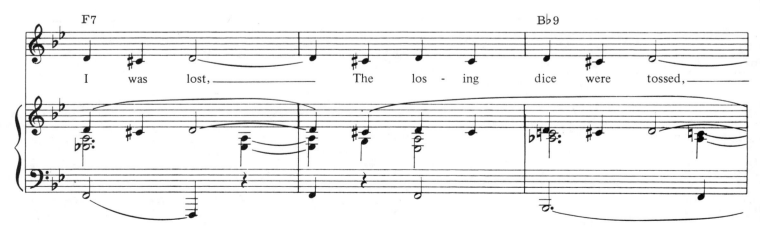

Life Is Just a Bowl of Cherries

Words and Music by LEW BROWN and RAY HENDERSON

Old Devil Moon

Words by E.Y. HARBURG
Music by BURTON LANE

214

Just when I think I'm _____ free as a dove _____ Old Dev - il Moon deep in your eyes blinds me with love.

eyes blinds me with love.

Rock-A-Bye Your Baby
with a Dixie Melody

Words by SAM M. LEWIS and JOE YOUNG
Music by JEAN SCHWARTZ

Verse:

Mam - my mine, _____ your lit - tle roll - in' stone that rolled a - way,_
An - y time _____ I hear a mam - my sing her babe to sleep,_

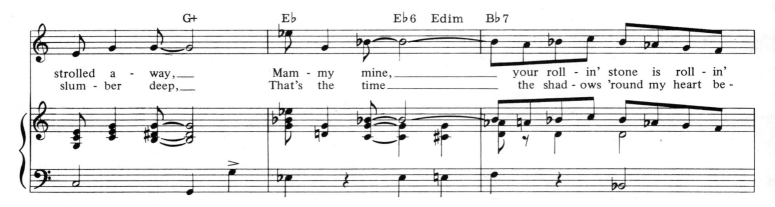

strolled a - way,_ Mam - my mine, _____ your roll - in' stone is roll - in'
slum - ber deep,_ That's the time _____ the shad - ows 'round my heart be -

home to - day,_ there to stay._ Just to see your
gin to creep,_ and I weep._ Won - der why I

Stormy Weather
(Keeps Rainin' All the Time)

Lyric by TED KOEHLER
Music by HAROLD ARLEN

Slow Lament

Don't know why_____ there's no sun up in the sky, Storm-y Weath-er,_____

Since my {man/gal} and I____ ain't to-geth-er,_____ keeps rain-in' all____ the time._____

Life is bare,_____ gloom and mis-'ry ev-'ry-where, Storm-y Weath-er,_____

Just can't get my poor— self to-geth-er,_____ I'm wea-ry all__ the time,_____ the

time,_____ So wea-ry all__ the time._____ When { he she } went a-way__ the blues walked

in and met me. If { he she } stays a-way__ old rock-in' chair will get me.

All I do is pray__ the Lord a-bove will let me walk in the sun once

more. Can't go on, _____ ev-'ry-thing I had is gone, Storm-y

Weath - er, _____ Since my {man/gal} and I _____ ain't to - geth - er, _____

keeps rain - in' all _____ the time, _____ keeps rain - in' all _____ the

time. _____ Don't know time. _____

224

What Now My Love
(Original French Title: "Et Maintenant")

Original French Lyric by PIERRE DELANOE
Music by GILBERT BECAUD
English Adaptation by CARL SIGMAN

226

my soul._____ What Now My
or die._____ What Now My
trop fort._____
me tuent._____ Je n'ai vrai-

Et Main - te -

Love _____ Now there is noth - ing____ On - ly my last____
ment_____ plus rien a fai - re____ Je n'ai vrai - ment____

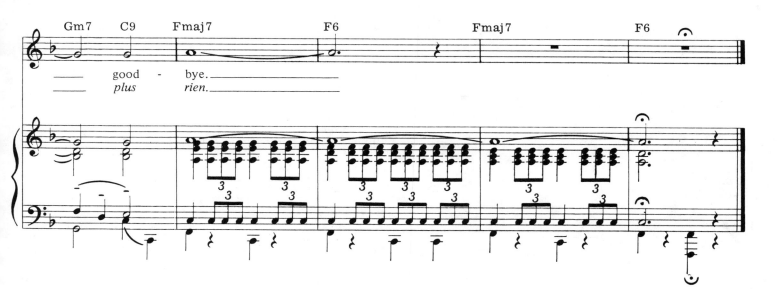

____ good - bye.
____ *plus rien.____*

San Francisco

Words by GUS KAHN
Music by BRONISLAU KAPER and WALTER JURMANN

228

Oth - er plac - es on - ly make me love you best

Tell me you're the heart of all the gold - en west

San Fran - cis - co wel - come me home____ a - gain

I'm com - ing home____ to go roam - ing no more. more.____

Singin' in the Rain

Words by ARTHUR FREED
Music by NACIO HERB BROWN

Sing - in' In The Rain, Just Sing - in' In The Rain. What a

glo - ri - ous feel - ing I'm hap - py a - gain, I'm

laugh - ing at clouds So dark up a - bove, The

sun's _____ in my heart _____ And I'm read - y for love. Let the

storm - y clouds chase Ev - 'ry - one _____ from the place, Come

on _____ with the rain, I've a smile _____ on my face. I'll

walk down the lane With a hap - py re - frain, And

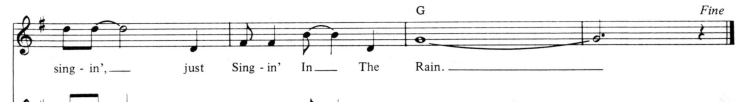

G   *Fine*

sing - in', ___ just Sing - in' In __ The __ Rain. _____

Eb7   **G**

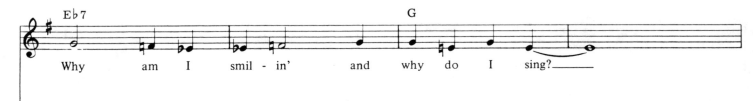

Why am I smil - in' and why do I sing? ___

Eb7   **G**

Why does De - cem - ber seem sun - ny as Spring? ___

Why do I get up each morn - ing to start _____

Hap - py and het up with joy in my heart? _____

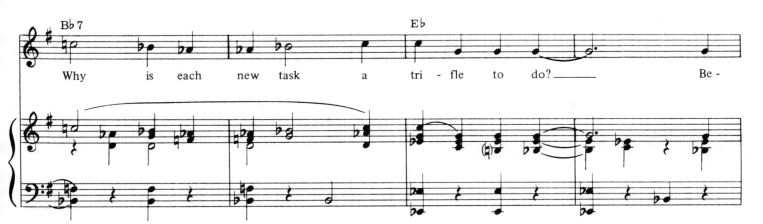

Why is each new task a tri - fle to do? _____ Be -

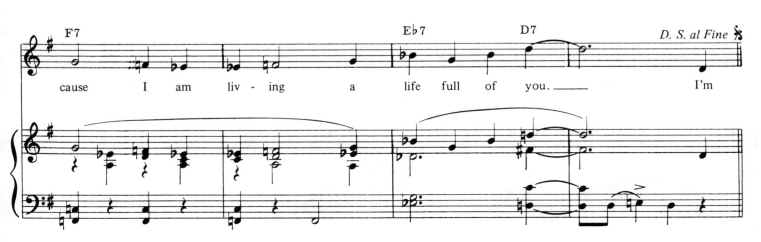

D. S. al Fine 𝄋

cause I am liv - ing a life full of you. _____ I'm

Smile

Words by JOHN TURNER and GEOFFREY PARSONS
Music by CHARLES CHAPLIN

That's Entertainment

Words by HOWARD DIETZ
Music by ARTHUR SCHWARTZ

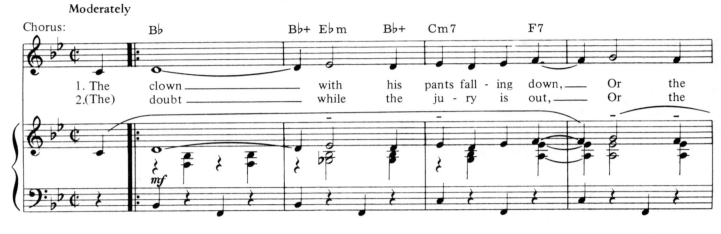

1. The clown _____ with his pants fall-ing down, _____ Or the
2. (The) doubt _____ while the ju-ry is out, _____ Or the

dance _____ that's a dream of ro-mance, _____ Or the
thrill _____ when they're read-ing the will, _____ Or the

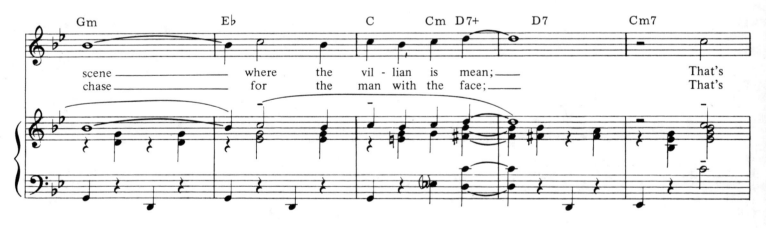

scene _____ where the vil-lian is mean; _____ That's
chase _____ for the man with the face; _____ That's

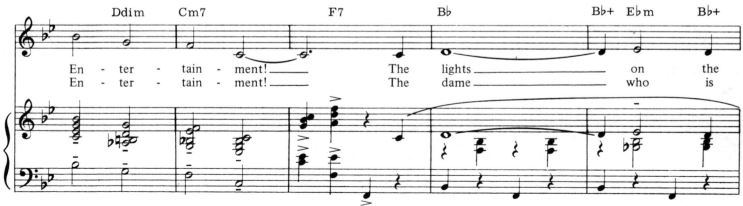

En-ter-tain-ment! _____ The lights _____ on the
En-ter-tain-ment! _____ The dame _____ who is

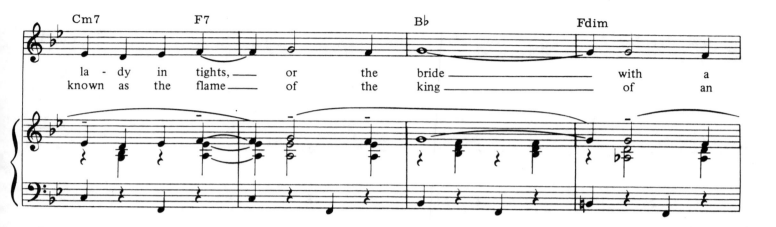

la - dy in tights, ___ or the bride ___ with a
known as the flame ___ of the king ___ of an

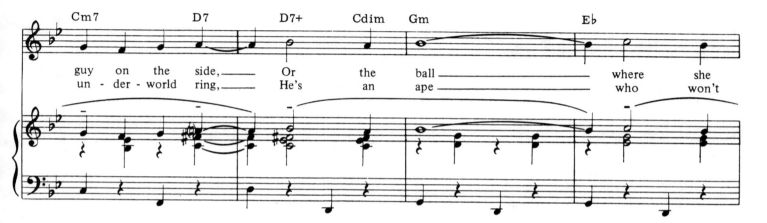

guy on the side, ___ Or the ball ___ where she
un - der - world ring, ___ He's an ape ___ who she won't

gives him her all, ___ That's En - ter - tain - ment!
let her es - cape, ___ That's En - ter - tain - ment!

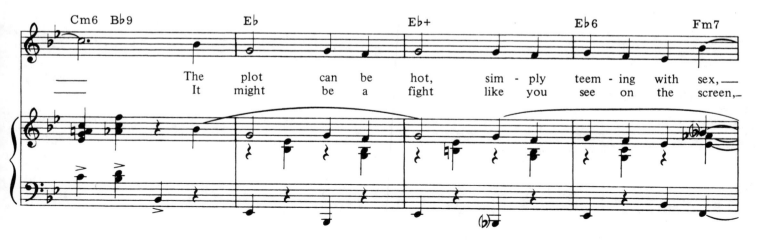

___ The plot can be hot, sim - ply teem - ing with sex, ___
___ It might be a fight like you see on the screen, ___

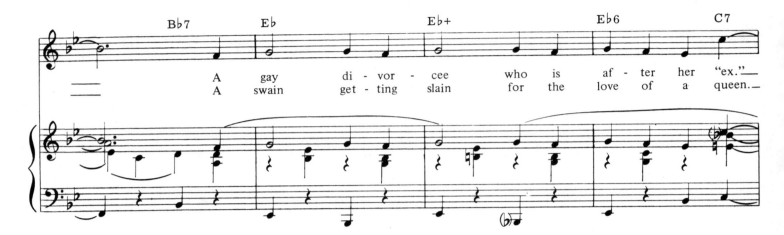

A gay di - vor - cee who is af - ter her "ex."
A swain get - ting slain who for the love of a queen.

It can be oe - di - pus rex
Some great Shake - spear - e - an scene

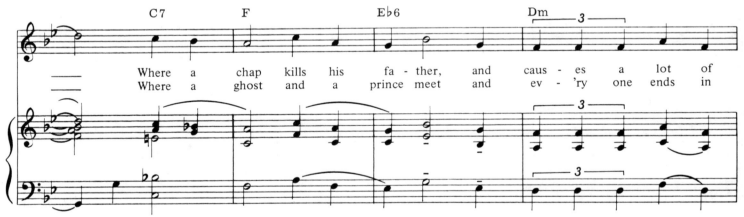

Where a chap kills his fa - ther, and caus - es a lot of
Where a ghost and a prince meet and ev - 'ry one ends in

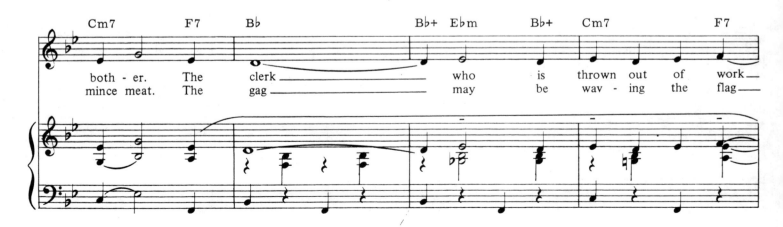

both - er. The clerk who is thrown out of work
mince meat. The gag may be wav - ing the flag

239

This Can't Be Love

Words by LORENZ HART
Music by RICHARD RODGERS

beat! This is too sweet to

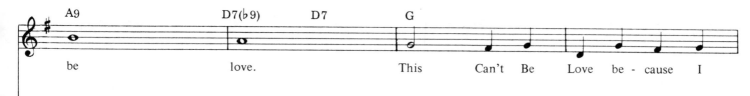

be love. This Can't Be Love be-cause I

feel so well;____ But still I love to look____ in your

eyes._____ eyes._____

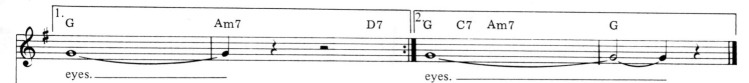

Through the Years

Words by EDWARD HEYMAN
Music by VINCENT YOUMANS

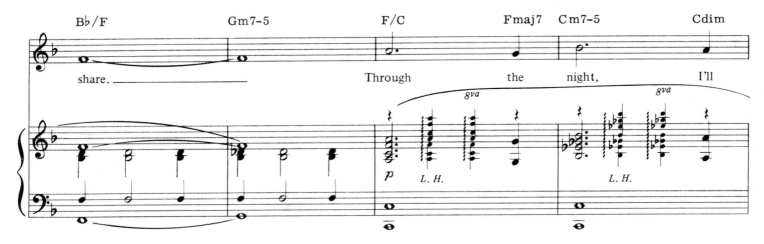

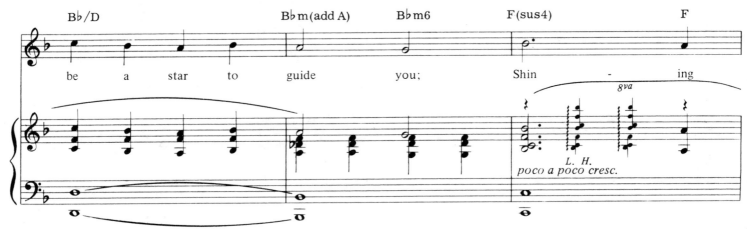

When You're Smiling
(The Whole World Smiles with You)

Words and Music by MARK FISHER,
JOE GOODWIN and LARRY SHAY

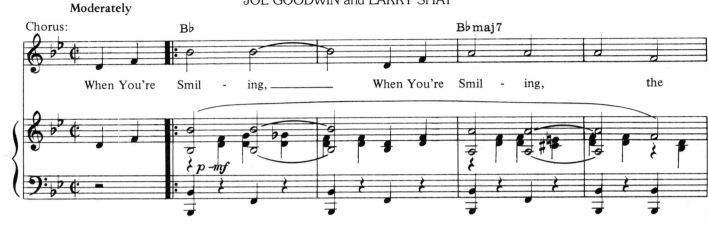

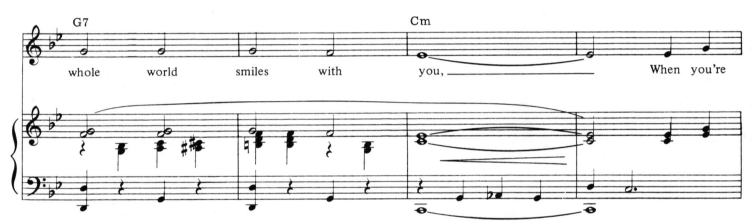

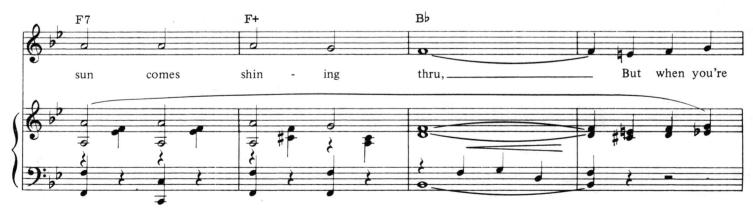

cry - ing _____ you bring on the rain, ____ So stop your

sigh - ing _____ be hap - py a - gain, ____ Keep on smil - ing _____

____ 'cause When You're Smil - ing, _____ _____ The whole world smiles with

you. _____ When You're   you. _____

You Go to My Head

Words by HAVEN GILLESPIE
Music by J. FRED COOTS

You Go To My Head_ like a sip of spar-kling

Bur-gun-dy brew_ and I find the ver-y men-tion of you_

like the kick-er in a ju-lep or two.___ The

thrill of the thought_ that you might give a thought_ to my

plea casts a spell o - ver me.___ Still I say to my - self, "Get a

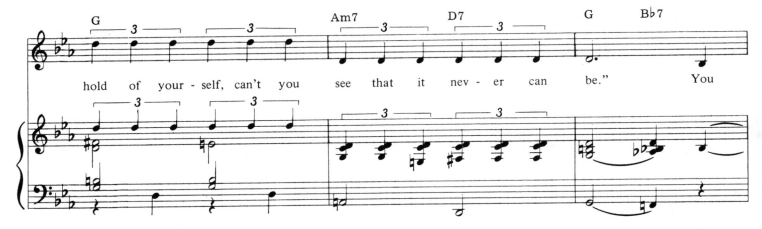

hold of your - self, can't you see that it nev - er can be." You

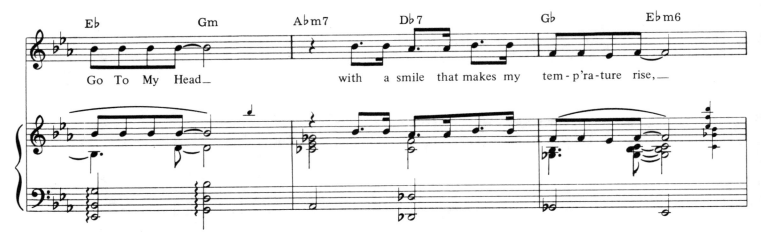

Go To My Head___ with a smile that makes my tem - p'ra - ture rise,___

like a sum - mer with a thou - sand Ju - lys,___ You in - tox - i - cate my

soul with your eyes._____ Tho' I'm cer - tain that this heart of mine_

has - n't a ghost of a chance in this cra - zy ro - mance,_____

You Go To My Head._____ You Go To My

Head._____ You Head._____

Little Girl Blue

Words by LORENZ HART
Music by RICHARD RODGERS

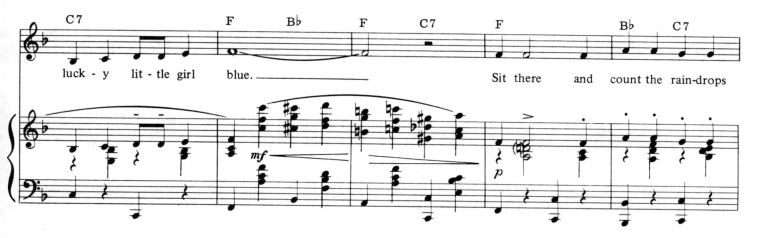

luck - y lit - tle girl blue._____ Sit there and count the rain-drops

fall - ing on you. It's time you knew, all you can

count on is the rain-drops That fall on lit - tle girl blue._____ No use, old

girl, you may as well sur - ren - der, Your hope is get - ting

The cir - cus tent was strung _____ with ev - 'ry star in the

sky A - bove the ring _____ I loved so well; _____

Now the young world has grown old, _____

Gone are the tin - sel and gold. _____

D. S. al Fine 𝄋

255

Comes Once in a Lifetime

Words by BETTY COMDEN and ADOLPH GREEN
Music by JULE STYNE

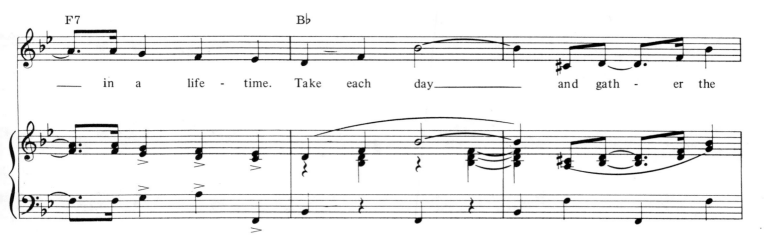

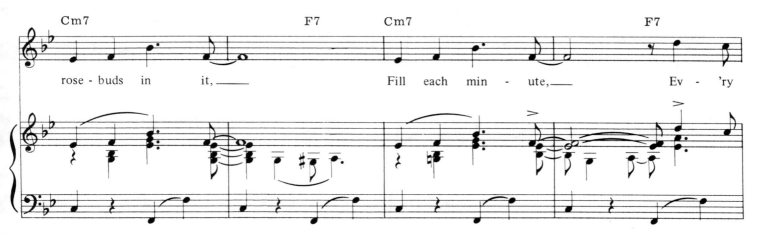

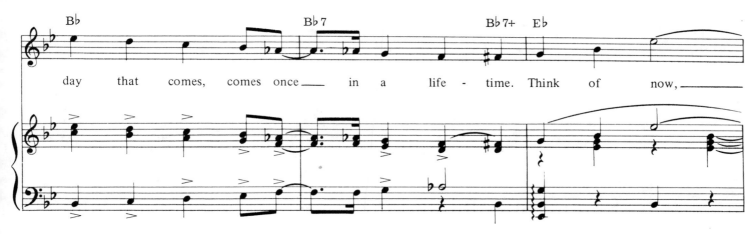

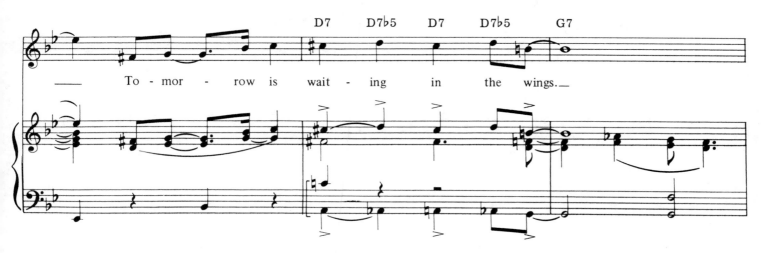

Who knows what it brings?— While the fu - ture waits,— the

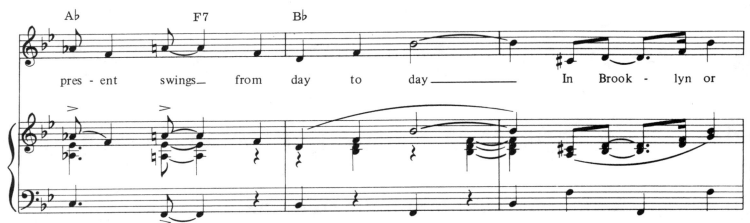

pres - ent swings— from day to day____ In Brook - lyn or

Chi - na 'cross the bay.— On - ly once comes this par - tic-

____ u - lar sky, On - ly once these pre - cious hou - rs will fly, On - ly

once in a life-time to-day comes by,____ So live, live,

live, to - day.____

day,_____ Let's live to - day._____

Judy with her mother, Ethel (Milne) Gumm

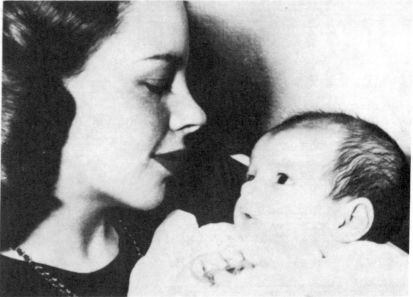

Judy with baby Liza

Frances Ethel Gumm (better known as *Judy Garland*) made her stage debut at three years of age.

JUDY GARLAND:
FAMILY SONGS

"If she (Judy) was happy, she wasn't just happy. She was ecstatic. And when she was sad, she was sadder than anyone."
James Mason at Judy's funeral.

Judy

Words and Music by HOAGY CARMICHAEL and SAMMY LERNER

Chorus:

If her voice can bring ev-'ry hope of the spring, That's Ju-dy,— my

Ju-dy,— If her eyes say "yes" but you're wrong in your guess, That's Ju-dy,— my

Ju-dy.— If you hear her call in a soft south-ern drawl,"Hi! strang-er!" That's dan-ger;—

If you're smart,— watch your heart— She'll up-set 'most an-y fel-low's ap-ple cart.— In a

Liza
(All the Clouds'll Roll Away)

Words and Music by GEORGE GERSHWIN,
IRA GERSHWIN and GUS KAHN

Happiness Is a Thing Called Joe

Words by E.Y. HARBURG
Music by HAROLD ARLEN

Lorna

Words by JOHNNY MERCER
Music by MORT LINDSEY

Slowly

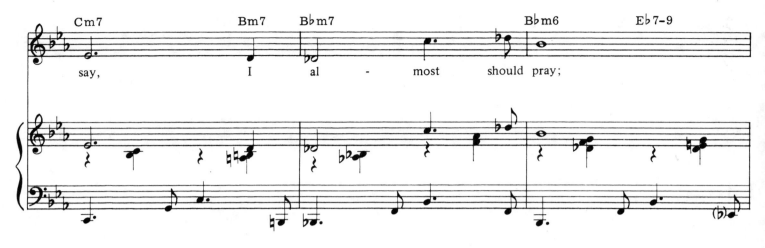

say, I al - most should pray;

Pray for the day_____ I can shout from the

roof - tops; Lor - na loves me

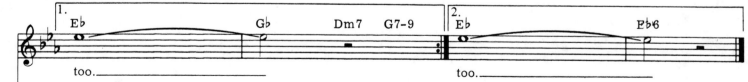

too._____ too._____

JUDY GARLAND FILMOGRAPHY

SHORT SUBJECTS

THE BIG REVUE (1929), 2 reels, a Mayfair production
with the Meglin Kiddies. Judy and her sisters
sang *"That's the Good Old Sunny South."*

A HOLIDAY IN STORYLAND (1930), a First National Vitaphone Short
with the Vitaphone Kiddies. Judy sang *"Blue Butterfly."*

THE WEDDING OF JACK AND JILL (1930), a First National Vitaphone
short with the Vitaphone Kidies. Judy sang *"Hang on to a
Rainbow."*

BUBBLES (1930), a First National Vitaphone Short
with the Vitaphone Kiddies. Judy sang *"Lady Luck."*

LA FIESTA DE SANTA BARBARA (1935), 2 reels, MGM
Directed by Louis Lewin
Judy sang with her sisters *"La Cucaracha."*

EVERY SUNDAY (1936), MGM
Directed by Felix Feist
with Judy Garland as Judy, Deanna Durbin and Sid Silvers
Judy sang *"Americana"*, and a verse to it by Roger Edens
(*"Waltz with a Swing"*)

WE MUST HAVE MUSIC (1942), MGM
A short about MGM's Music Department.
Judy's song, *"We Must Have Music"* was cut from *"Ziegfeld
Girl."*

FEATURE FILMS

PIGSKIN PARADE (1936), 20th Century Fox
Directed by David Butler
Associate Producer: Bogart Rogers
Screenplay by Harry Tugend, Jack Yellen and William Conselman
Original Story by Art Sheekman, Nat Perrin and Mark Kelly
Musical Direction by David Buttolph
Costumes by Gwen Wakeling
Photography by Arthur Miller
Film Editing by Irene Morra
CAST
Stuart Erwin, Patsy Kelly, Jack Haley, The Yacht Club Boys, Johnny Downs, Betty Grable,
Arline Judge, Dixie Dunbar, Judy Garland (as Sairy Dodd), Anthony "Tony" Martin, Grady
Sutton, Fred Kohler, Jr., Elisha Cook, Jr., Eddie Nugent, Julius Tannen, Pat Flaherty, Si Jenks,
Lynn Bari, George Offerman, Jr., Maurice Cass, Douglas Wood, Alan Ladd.

JUDY'S SONGS - All written by Sidney Mitchell & Lew Pollack
It's Love I'm After
The Balboa
The Texas Tornado
Hold That Bulldog (cut before release)

*"Also in the newcomer category is Judy Garland, about twelve or thirteen now, about whom the West
Coast has been enthusing as a vocal find . . . She's cute, not too pretty, but a pleasingly fetching
personality, who certainly knows how to sell a pop."*
The New York Times

BROADWAY MELODY OF 1938 (1937) - MGM

Directed by Roy Del Ruth
Produced by Jack Cummings
Screenplay by Jack McGowan
Original Story by Jack McGowan and Sid Silvers
Music and Lyrics by Nacio Herb Brown and Arthur Freed
Dance Direction by Dave Gould
Musical Direction by George Stoll
Arrangements by Roger Edens
Costumes by Adrian
Photography by William Daniels
Film Editiong by Blanche Sewell
Art Direction by Cedric Gibbons
CAST
Robert Taylor, Eleanor Powell, George Murphy, Binnie Barnes, Buddy Ebsen, Sophie Tucker, Judy Garland (as Betty Clayton), Charles Igor Gorin, Raymond Walburn, Robert Benchley, Willie Howard, Esther Howard, Grace Hayle, Billy Gilbert, Charles Grapewin, Robert Wildhack, Barnett Parker, Helen Troy.
JUDY'S SONGS
(Dear Mr. Gable) You Made Me Love You
Everybody Sing
Yours and Mine and Finale

"A girl named Judy Garland . . . does a heart-rending song about her unrequited love for Clark Gable, which the audience seemed to like."
The New York Herald Tribune (M. Tazelaar)

THOROUGHBREDS DON'T CRY (1937) - MGM

Produced by Harry Rapf
Directed by Alfred E. Green
Screenplay by Lawrence Hazard
Original Story by Eleanore Griffin and J. Walter Ruben
Music and Lyric by Nacio Herb Brown and Arthur Freed
Musical Direction by William Axt
Costumes by Dolly Tree
Photography by Leonard Smith
Film Editing by Elmo Vernon
CAST
Judy Garland (as Cricket West), Mickey Rooney, Sophie Tucker, C. Aubrey Smith, Ronald Sinclair, Helen Troy, Forrester Harvey, Frankie Darro, Charles D. Brown, Henry Kolker.
JUDY'S SONGS
Got a Pair of New Shoes
Sun Showers (cut before release)

"Judy Garland is the puppy-love interest who tosses off some scorchy rhythm - singing ...."
The New York Times (B. Crowther)

EVERYBODY SING (1938) - MGM

Produced by Harry Rapf
Directed by Edwin L. Marin
Screenplay by Florence Ryerson and Edgar Woolf
Original Story by Florence Ryerson and Edgar Allan Woolf
Additional Dialogue by James Gruen
Musical Arrangements by Roger Edens
Music and Lyrics by Gus Kahn, Bronislav Kaper, Walter Jurmann,
    Harry Ruby and Bert Kalmar
Costumes by Dolly Tree
Photography by Joseph Ruttenberg

CAST

Allan Jones, Fanny Brice, Judy Garland (as Judy Bellaire), Billie Burke, Lynne Carver, Reginald Owen, Reginald Gardiner, Helen Troy, Monty Woolley, Andrew Tombes, Henry Armetta.

JUDY'S SONGS

Down on Melody Farm
Swing, Mr, Mendelssohn, Swing
Why? Because (with Fanny Brice)
Swing Low, Sweet Chariot
Bus Sequence

"... Judy Garland of the rhythm, writin' and 'rithmetic age is a superb vocal technician, despite her not exactly underemphasized immaturity ... "

The New York Times (B. Crowther)

LISTEN, DARLING (1938) - MGM

Produced by Jack Cummings
Directed by Edwin L. Marin
Screenplay by Elaine Ryan and Anne Morrison Chapin
Original Story by Katherine Brush
Musical Direction by George Stoll
Arrangements by Roger Edens
Music and Lyrics by Joseph McCarthy, Milton Ager, Al Lewis,
      Al Hoffman, Murray Mencher and James Hanley
Costumes by Dolly Tree
Photography by Charles Lawton, Jr.
Art Direction by Cedric Gibbons
Film Editiong by Blanche Sewell

CAST

Freddie Bartholomew, Judy Garland (as Pinkie Wingate), Mary Astor, Walter Pidgeon, Alan Hale, Charley Grapewin, Scotty Beckett, Gene Lockhart, Barnett Parker, Byron Foulger, Bobbie Stebbins

JUDY'S SONGS

Zing! Went the Strings of My Heart
Ten Pins in the Sky
On the Bumpy Road to Love

"... Besides being a charming little miss, Judy Garland has a fresh young voice, which she uses happily on "Zing! Went the String of My Heart", "On the Bumpy Road to Love" and "Ten Pins in the Sky.""

LOVE FINDS ANDY HARDY (1938) - MGM

Produced by Lou Ostrow
Directed by George B. Seitz
Screenplay by William Ludwig from the Stories by
      Vivien R. Bretherton
Based on Characters Created by Aurania Rouverol
Musical Score by David Snell
Vocal Arrangements by Roger Edens
Songs by Mack Gordon, Harry Revel and Roger Edens
Costumes by Jeanne
Photography by Lester White
Film Editing by Ben Lewis

CAST

Lewis Stone, Mickey Rooney, Judy Garland (as Betsy Booth), Cecilia Parker, Fay Holden, Ann Rutherford, Betty Ross Clark, Lana Turner, Marie Blake, Don Castle, Gene Reynolds, Mary Howard, George Breakston, Raymond Hatton, Frank Darien, Rand Brooks, Erville Alderson.

JUDY'S SONGS

Meet the Beat of My Heart   *In Between*
It Never Rains, But it Pours   *Bei Mir Bist Du Schoen* (cut before release)

"If the comedy falters, it is because an ill-advised attempt has been made to bring in some musical numbers in the ending. Judy Garland sings them and they are catchy enough pieces but they have no proper place in this sort of show."

The New York Herald Tribune (H. Barnes)

THE WIZARD OF OZ (1939) - MGM Technicolor
    Produced by Mervyn LeRoy
    Directed by Victor Fleming
    Screenplay by Noel Langley, Florence Ryerson & Edgar Woolf
    Adapted from the Book by L. Frank Baum
    Color by Technicolor, opening and closing scenes in Sepia
    Music Score by Herbert Stothart (and Roger Edens)
    Songs by Harold Arlen and E.Y. Harburg
    Musical Numbers Staged by Bobby Connolly
    Art Direction by Cedric Gibbons and William A. Horning
    Sets by Edwin B. Willis
    Special Effects by Arnold Gillespie
    Associate Conductor, George Stoll
    Orchestral and Vocal Arrangements by George Bassman, Murray Cutter,
        Paul Marquardt, Ken Darby and Roger Edens
    Character Make-up by Jack Dawn
    Photography by Harold Rosson
    Film Editing by Blanche Sewell
    CAST
        Judy Garland (as Dorothy Gale), Frank Morgan, Ray Bolger, Bert Lahr, Jack Haley, Billie Burke, Margaret Hamilton, Charley Grapewin, Clara Blandick, Pat Walshe, Jerry Maren, Toto, The Singer Midgets.

    JUDY'S SONGS
        Over the Rainbow
        Follow the Yellow Brick Road
        We're Off to See the Wizard
        Munchkinland
        The Jitterbug; Laugh a Day Away (cut before release)

"Judy Garland is perfectly cast as Dorothy. She is as clever a little actress as she is a singer, and her special style of vocalizing is ideally adapted to the music of the picture."
            The New York Daily News (Kate Cameron)

BABES IN ARMS (1939) - MGM
    Produced by Arthur Freed
    Directed by Busby Berkeley
    Screenplay by Jack McGowan and Kay Van Riper
    Bassed on the Broadway Musical by Richard Rodgers and Lorenz Hart
    Music and Lyrics by Richard Rodgers and Lorenz Hart
    Musical Direction by George Stoll
    Other Songs by Arthur Freed, Nacio Herb Brown, Gus Arnheim,
        Abe Lyman, E.Y. Harburg and Harold Arlen.
    Orchestration by Conrad Salinger
    Musical Adaption by Roger Edens
    Costumes by Dolly Tree
    Art Direction by Cedric Gibbons
    Photography by Ray June
    Film Editing by Frank Sullivan.
    CAST
        Mickey Rooney, Judy Garland (as Patsy Barton), Charles Winninger, Guy Kibbee, June Preisser, Grace Hayes, Betty Jaynes, Douglas McPhail, Rand Brooks, Leni Lynn, John Sheffield, Henry Hull, Barnett Parker, Ann Shoemaker, Margaret Hamilton, Joseph Crehan, George McKay, Lelah Tyler, Lon McCallister.
    JUDY'S SONGS

I Cried for You	*Figaro*
Good Morning	*Broadway Rhythm*
Where or When	*Minstrel Show*
God's Country	*Oh, Susanna*
Babes in Arms	*I'm Just Wild About Harry*
I Like Opera; I Like Swing	*My Day*

". . . a brightly entertaining screen version of the Rodgers and Hart legit musical. Perked up by . . . Judy Garland's simply swell sense of swing . . ."
            The New York Post (I. Thirer)

ANDY HARDY MEETS DEBUTANTE (1940) - MGM

Produced by J.J. Cohn
Directed by George B. Seitz
Screenplay by Annalee Whitmore and Thomas Seller
Based on Characters Created by Aurania Rouverol
Songs; *"Alone"* by Arthur Freed and Nacio Herb Brown
        "I'm Nobody's Baby" by Lester Santley, Benny Davis
        and Milton Ager
Musical Score by David Snell
Musical Arrangements by George Stoll
Musical Arrangements by Roger Edens
Musical Conductor, George Stoll
Photography by Sidney Wager, and Charles Lawton, Jr.
Costumes by Dolly Tree
Film Editing by Harold F. Kress

CAST

Lewis Stone, Mickey Rooney, Judy Garland (as Betsy Booth), Cecilia Parker, Fay Holden, Ann Rutherford, Diana Lewis, Sara Haden, George Breakston, George Lessey, Harry Tyler, Gladys Blake, Addison Richards, Cy Kendall.

JUDY'S SONGS

Alone
I'm Nobody's Baby
All I Do is Dream of You
Buds Won't Bud (cut before release)

"Some of Cinemactor Stone's heartiest chuckles may be explained by the fact that seventeen-year-old Judy Garland, growing prettier by the picture, and armed for this one with two good songs, "Alone" and "I'm Nobody's Baby," treats Mickey with a dose of his own medicine."

Time Magazine

STRIKE UP THE BAND (1940) - MGM

Produced by Arthur Freed
Directed by Busby Berkeley
Screenplay by John Monks, Jr. and Fred Finklehoffe
Music and Lyrics by Roger Edens and Arthur Freed, George
        and Ira Gershwin
Chorals and Orchestrations by Conrad Salinger and Leo Arnaud
Musical Direction by George Stoll
Photography by Ray June
Film Editing by Ben Lewis

CAST

Mickey Rooney, Judy Garland (as Mary Holden), June Preisser, William Tracy, Larry Nunn, Margaret Early, Enid Bennett, Ann Shoemaker, Sarah Edwards, Milton Kibbee, Virginia Brissac, Helen Jerome Eddy, Francis Pierlot, Paul Whiteman and his Orchestra.

JUDY'S SONGS

Nobody
Drummer Boy
Do the La Conga
Nell of New Rochelle
Our Love Affair
Strike Up the Band
My Wonderful One, Let's Dance
The Dear Gay Nineties
Heaven Will Protect the Working Girl

"Miss Garland particularly achieves rank in this picture as one of the screen's greatest personalities. Here she is for the first time in the full bloom and charm which is beyond childhood, as versatile in acting as she is excellent in song - a striking figure, and a most oomphish one in the wild abandon of the "La Conga" number."

Hollywood Reporter, 9/13/40

LITTLE NELLIE KELLY (1940) - MGM

Produced by Arthur Freed
Directed by Norman Taurog
Screenplay by Jack McGowan
Based on the Musical Comedy by George M. Cohan
Song, *"Singin' in the Rain"* by Arthur Freed and Nacio Herb Brown
Musical Adaptation by Roger Edens
Musical Direction by George Stoll
Costumes by Dolly Tree
Photography by Ray June
Film Editing by Frederick Y. Smith

CAST

Judy Garland (as Nellie Kelly and her mother), George Murphy, Charles Winninger, Douglas MacPhail, Arthur Shields, James Burke, Robert Homans, Thomas Dillon, Rita Page, Henry Blair, Forrester Harvey, Frederick Worlock.

JUDY'S SONGS

A Pretty Girl Milking Her Cow
It's a Great Day for the Irish
Singin' in the Rain
Danny Boy (cut before release)

"Judy Garland in the double role . . . does her best, but even her beguiling exuberance and her sweet way with a ballad cannot entirely overcome the deficiencies of the story."

The New York Daily News (K. Cameron)

ZIEGFELD GIRL (1941) - MGM

Produced by Pandro S. Berman
Directed by Robert Z. Leonard
Screenplay by Marguerite Roberts and Sonya Levien
Original Story by William Anthony Mcguire
Musical Numbers Directed by Busby Berkeley
Musical Direction by George Stoll
Orchestration and Vocals by Leo Arnaud, George Bassman
    and Conrad Salinger
Music and Lyrics by Nacio Herb Brown, Gus Kahn, Roger Edens, Ralph Freed,
    Harry Carroll, Joseph McCarthy, Edward Gallagher,
    Al Shean, John Schonberger, Richard Coburn, Vincent
    Rose, Harold Adamson and Walter Donaldson
Costumes by Adrian
Make-up by Jack Dawn
Art Direction by Cedric Gibbons
Sets by Edwin B. Willis
Sound by Douglas Shearer
Photography by Ray June
Film Editing by Blanche Sewell

CAST

James Stewart, Judy Garland (as Susan Gallagher), Hedy Lamarr, Lana Turner, Jackie Cooper, Tony Martin, Ian Hunter, Charles Winninger, Edward Everett Horton, Philip Dorn, Paul Kelly, Eve Arden, Dan Dailey, Jr., Mae Busch, Al Shean, Fay Holden, Rose Hobart, Felix Bressart, Bernard Nedell, Renie Riano, Josephine Whittell, Jean Wallace, Myrna Dell, Georgia Carroll, Leslie Brooks, Claire James, Louise LaPlanche, Frances Gladwin, Patricia Dane, Anya Taranda.

JUDY'S SONGS

Minnie from Trinidad
I'm Always Chasing Rainbows
Laugh? I Thought I'd Split My Sides
We Must Have Music (cut before release)

". . . Miss Garland warbles a torrid tropical tune, "Minnie from Trinidad" with true professional gusto."

Time Magazine

"Judy Garland is especially good as a youngster who becomes a star under a strict code of showmanship . . ."

The New York Herald Tribune (H. Barnes)

LIFE BEGINS FOR ANDY HARDY (1941) - MGM

Produced by J.J. Cohn
Directed by George B. Seitz
Screenplay by Agnes Christine Johnston
Based on Characters Created by Aurania Rouverol
Musical Direction by George Stoll
Costumes by Kalloch
Art Direction by Cedric Gibbons
Photography by Lester White
Film Editing by Elmo Vernon

CAST

Lewis Stone, Mickey Rooney, Judy Garland (as Betsy Booth), Fay Holden, Ann Rutherford, Sara Haden, Patricia Dane, Ray McDonald, George Breakston, Pierre Watkin.

JUDY'S SONGS (All were cut before release)

Easy to Love
The Rosary
Abide With Me
America

"Judy Garland's talent is by no means taxed in the role of Betsy."
The New York Times (T.M.P.)

BABES ON BROADWAY (1941) - MGM

Produced by Arthur Freed
Directed by Busby Berkeley
Screenplay by Fred Finklehoffe and Elaine Ryan
Musical Adaptation by Roger Edens
Songs by E.Y. Harburg, Burton Lane, Ralph Freed,
        Roger Edens, Harold Rome
Musical Direction by George Stoll
Vocals and Orchestrations by Leo Arnaud, George Bassman and
        Conrad Salinger
Costumes by Kalloch
Photography by Lester White
Film Editing by Frederick Y. Smith

CAST

Mickey Rooney, Judy Garland (as Penny Morris), Fay Bainter, Virginia Weidler, Ray McDonald, Richard Quine, Donald Meek, James Gleason, Emma Dunn, Frederick Burton, Cliff Clark, Alexander Woollcott, William Post, Jr., Donna Reed, Luis Alberni, Joe Yule.

JUDY'S SONGS

Babes on Broadway
I'm a Yankee Doodle Dandy
How About You
Mary is a Grand Old Name
I've Got Rings on My Fingers
Bombshell from Brazil
Hoe Down
Chin Up! Cheerio! Carry On!
Minstrel Show
Franklin D. Roosevelt Jones
Waiting for the Robert E. Lee
Blackout Over Broadway

". . . Miss Garland, now nineteen and wise to her co-star's propensity for stealing scenes, neatly takes the picture away from him. Rooney cannot sing but Judy Garland can and proves it pleasantly with such sure-fire numbers as "Waiting for the Robert E. Lee", "Franklin D. Roosevelt Jones" and a new tune called "Hoe Down."

Time Magazine

FOR ME AND MY GAL (1942) - MGM
Produced by Arthur Freed
Directed by Busby Berkeley
Screenplay by Richard Sherman, Fred Finklehoffe and Sid Silvers
Original Story by Howard Emmett Rogers
Musical Adaptation by Roger Edens
Dance Direction by Bobby Connolly
Vocals and Orchestration by Conrad Salinger,
    George Bassman and Leo Arnaud
Costumes by Kalloch
Photographed by William Daniels
Film Editing by Ben Lewis
CAST
    Judy Garland (as Jo Hayden), George Murphy, Gene Kelly, Marta Eggerth, Ben Blue, Richard Quine, Keenan Wynn, Horace McNally, Lucille Norman.
JUDY'S SONGS
    After You've Gone
    How Ya Gonna Keep 'Em Down on the Farm
    Ballin The Jack
    For Me and My Gal
    When You Wore A Tulip
    Where Do We Go From Here
    Don't Leave Me, Daddy
    It's A Long Way To Tipperary
    Smiles
    Pack Up Your Troubles
    Goodbye Broadway, Hello France
    Til We Meet Again

"Judy Garland continues to gain impressiveness as a persuasive and skillful actress, capable of getting audience heart-tugs as well as admiration for her singing and dancing. Her love moods as the two work out their ambition to make the vaudeville big-time in a story about stage ambition."

Variety 9/9/42

PRESENTING LILY MARS (1943) - MGM
Produced by Joseph Pasternak
Directed by Norman Taurog
Screenplay by Richard Connell and Gladys Lehman
Based on the novel by Booth Tarkington
Songs by Walter Jurmann, Paul Francis Webster, Merrill Pye,
    E.Y. Harburg, Burton Lane, Roger Edens
Musical Direction by George Stoll
Musical Adaptation by Roger Edens
Dance Direction by Ernst Matray
Gowns by Howard Shoup
Photographed by Joseph Ruttenberg
Film Editing by Albert Akst
CAST
    Judy Garland (as Lily Mars), Van Heflin, Fay Bainter, Richard Carlson, Spring Byington, Connie Gilchrist, Marta Eggerth, Ray McDonald, Leonid Kinskey, Annabelle Logan, Janet Chapman, Patricia Barker, Douglas Croft, Marilyn Maxwell, Tommy Dorsey and his orchestra, Bob Crosby and his orchestra, Charles Walters.
JUDY'S SONGS
    When I Look At You
    Tom, Tom, The Piper's Son
    Every Little Movement
    Broadway Rhythm
    Paging Mr. Greenback (cut before release)

"Miss Garland is fresh and pretty - she has a perky friendliness that is completely disarming. She is a gifted young lady."

The New York Times

GIRL CRAZY (1943) - MGM

Produced by Arthur Freed
Directed by Norman Taurog
Screenplay by Fred Finklehoffe
Original story by Guy Bolton and Jack McGowan
Music and Lyrics by George and Ira Gershwin
Musical Adaptation by Roger Edens
Musical Direction by George Stoll
Costumes by Irene
Orchestrations by Conrad Salinger, Axel Stordahl and Sy Oliver
Dance Direction by Charles Walters
Photographed by William Daniels and Robert Planck
Film Editing by Albert Akst

CAST

Mickey Rooney, Judy Garland (as Ginger Gray), Gil Stratton, Nancy Walker, June Allyson, Robert E. Strickland, Rags Ragland, Guy Kibbee, Frances Rafferty, Howard Freeman, Henry O'Neill, Sidney Miller, Sarah Edwards, William Bishop, Eve Whitney, Barbara Bedford, Hazel Brooks, Peter Lawford, Don Taylor, Bess Flowers, Georgia Carroll, Tommy Dorsey and his Orchestra.

JUDY'S SONGS

But Not for Me
Embraceable You
Could You Use Me
Bidin' My Time
I Got Rhythm

". . . Miss Garland's songs, such as "Bidin' My Time," should soothe even the most savage breast; of all the child prodigies of Hollywood, Miss Garland has outgrown her adolescence most gracefully, and still sings a song with an appealing sincerity which is downright irresistable."

The New York Times (T.S.)

THOUSANDS CHEER (1943) - MGM Technicolor

Produced by Joseph Pasternak
Directed by George Sidney
Screenplay by Paul Jarrico and Richard Collins
Based on their story "Private Miss Jones"
Musical Adaptation by Herbert Stothart
Costumes by Irene
Photographed by George Folsey
Film Editing by George Boemler

CAST

Kathryn Grayson, Gene Kelly, Mary Astor, Jose Iturbi, John Boles, Ben Blue, Dick Simmons, Frances Rafferty, Odette Myrtil, Mary Elliott, Frank Jenks, Wally Cassell, Frank Sully, Betty Jaynes.

GUEST STARS

Mickey Rooney, Judy Garland, Red Skelton, Eleanor Powell, Ann Sothern, Lucille Ball, Lena Horne, Virginia O'Brien, Marsha Hunt, Marilyn Maxwell, Frank Morgan, Donna Reed, June Allyson, Margaret O'Brien, Gloria DeHaven, Lionel Barrymore, John Conte, Sara Haden, Connie Gilchrist, Marta Linden, Kay Kyser and his Orchestra, Bob Crosby and his Orchestra, Benny Carter and his Band, Don Loper and Maxine Barrat.

JUDY'S SONGS

The Joint is Really Jumping by Ralph Blane and Hugh Martin

". . . Judy Garland is attractive as she gets Jose Iturbi to bang out some swing rhythms on the piano."

The New York Herald Tribune (Howard Barnes)

MEET ME IN ST. LOUIS (1944) - MGM Technicolor
Produced by Arthur Freed
Directed by Vincente Minnelli
Screenplay by Irving Brecher and Fred Finklehoffe
Based on Book by Sally Benson
Musical Adaptation by Roger Edens
Musical Direction by George Stoll
Orchestration by Conrad Salinger
Dance Direction by Charles Walters
Photography by George Folsey
Costumes by Sharaff
Film Editing by Albert Akst
New Songs by Hugh Martin and Ralph Blane

CAST
    Judy Garland (as Esther Smith), Margaret O'Brien, Mary Astor, Lucille Bremer, Tom Drake, Marjorie Main, Leon Ames, Harry Davenport, Joan Carroll, June Lockhart, Henry Daniels, Jr., Hugh Marlowe, Robert Sully, Chill Wills, Darryl Hickman, Donald Curtis, Mary Jo Ellis, Belle Mitchell, Victor Kilian.

JUDY'S SONGS
    The Boy Next Door
    Have Yourself a Merry Little Xmas
    The Trolley Song
    Meet Me in St. Louis, Louis
    Skip to My Lou
    Under the Bamboo Tree
    Over the Bannister
    Boys and Girls Like You and Me (cut before release)

"A charming movie, Miss Garland is full of gay exuberance as the second sister of the lot, and sings . . . with a rich voice that grows riper and more expressive in each new film. Her chortling of "The Trolley Song" puts fresh zip into that inescapable tune . . ."
                                    The New York Times (B. Crowther)

"'Meet Me in St. Louis' is a musical that even the deaf should enjoy."
                                    Time Magazine (J. Agee)

THE CLOCK (1945) - MGM
Produced by Arthur Freed
Directed by Vincente Minnelli
Screenplay by Robert Nathan and Joseph Schrank
From Original Story by Paul and Pauline Jarrico
Musical Score by George Bassman
Costumes by Irene and Marion Herwood Keyes
Special Effects by A. Arnold Gillespie
Photography by George Folsey
Film Editing by George White

CAST
    Judy Garland (as Alice Mayberry), Robert Walker, James Gleason, Keenan Wynn, Marshall Thompson, Lucile Gleason, Moyna MacGill, Ruth Brady, Chester Clute, Dick Elliott, Arthur Space, Ray Teal.

"In this film Miss Garland can handle every emotion in sight, in any size and shape, and the audience along with it."
                                    The Nation (James Agee)

THE HARVEY GIRLS (1946) - MGM

Produced by Arthur Freed
Directed by George Sidney
Screenplay by Edmund Beloin and Nathaniel Curtis
Additional Dialogue by Kay Van Riper
Based on the Book by Samuel Hopkins Adams
Songs by Johnny Mercer and Harry Warren
Orchestrations by Conrad Salinger
Musical Direction by Lennie Hayton
Vocal Arrangements by Kay Thompson
Musical Numbers Staged by Robert Alton
Photography by George Folsey
Film Editing by Albert Akst

CAST

Judy Garland (as Susan Bradley), John Hodiak, Ray Bolger, Angela Lansbury, Preston Foster, Virginia O'Brien, Marjorie Main, Kenny Baker, Cyd Charisse, Selena Royle, Catherine McLeod, Chill Wills, Ruth Brady, Jack Lambert, Horace McNally, Ben Carter, Ray Teal, Hazel Brooks, Bunny Waters, Peggy Maley, Jacqueline White, Eve Whitney.

JUDY'S SONGS

On the Atchison, Topeka and the Santa Fe
In the Valley Where the Evening Sun Goes Down
It's a Great Big World
Swing Your Partner Round and Round
Hayride (cut before release)
March of the Doagies (cut before release)
My Intuition (cut before release)

"Miss Garland doesn't seem as recklessly happy as she was in St. Louis, but she still appears to be having a good time."

Time Magazine

ZIEGFELD FOLLIES (1946) - MGM Technicolor

Produced by Arthur Freed
Directed by Vincente Minnelli
Songs by Harry Warren, Arthur Freed, George and Ira Gershwin,
    Ralph Blane, Hugh Martin, Earl Brent, Ralph Freed, Roger
    Edens, Philio Brahva, Douglas Furber, and Kay Thompson.
Musical Direction by Lennie Hayton
Orchestrations by Kay Thompson
Photography by George Folsey, Charles Rocher and Ray June
Costumes by Irene; designed by Irene Sharaff and Helen Rose
Dance Direction by Robert Alton
Film Editing by Albert Akst

CAST

Fred Astaire, Lucille Ball, Lucille Bremer, Fanny Brice, Judy Garland, Kathryn Grayson, Lena Horne, Gene Kelly, James Melton, Victor Moore, Red Skelton, Esther Williams, William Powell, Cyd Charisse, Marion Bell, Edward Arnold, Ray Teal, Naomi Childers, Hume Cronyn, William Frawley, Robert Lewis, Harriet Lee, Rex Evans, Bunin Puppets

JUDY'S SONG

A Great Lady has an Interview, written by Roger Edens and Kay Thompson, staged by Charles Walters and directed by Vincente Minnelli.

"In "A Great Lady Has An Interview", Judy Garland, with six leading men, displays an unexpected flair for occupational satire."

Newsweek

TILL THE CLOUDS ROLL BY (1946) - MGM Technicolor

Produced by Arthur Freed
Directed by Richard Whorf
Screenplay by Myles Connolly and Jean Holloway
Story by Guy Bolton, adapted by George Wells
Based on the life and music of Jerome Kern
Musical Direction by Lennie Hayton
Orchestrations by Conrad Salinger
Vocal Arrangements by Kay Thompson
Musical Numbers staged and directed by Robert Alton
Photographed by Harry Stradling and George Folsey
Costumes supervised by Irene; designed by Helen Rose
Film Editing by Albert Akst

CAST

Robert Walker, Judy Garland (as Marilyn Miller), Lucille Bremer, Van Heflin, Dorothy Patrick, Mary Nash, Paul Langton, Joan Wells, Harry Hayden and William "Bill" Phillips, with June Allyson, Kathryn Grayson, Lena Horne, Van Johnson, Angela Lansbury, Gower Champion, Cyd Charisse, Tony Martin, Ray McDonald, Virginia O'Brien, Dinah Shore, Frank Sinatra, Caleb Peterson, and The Wilde Twins.

JUDY'S SONGS

Who? (directed by Vincente Minnelli)
Look For The Silver Lining (directed by Vincente Minnelli)
D'ye Love Me? (cut before release)

"Judy Garland is charming as the late Marilyn Miller and still more charming when she sings "Who".
Time Magazine

THE PIRATE (1948), MGM Technicolor

Produced by Arthur Freed
Directed by Vincente Minnelli
Screenplay by Albert Hackett and Frances Goodrich
From the play by S.N. Behrman
Songs by Cole Porter
Musical Direction by Lennie Hayton
Instrumental Arrangements by Conrad Salinger
Vocal Arrangements by Kay Thompson, Robert Tucker and Roger Edens
Dance Direction by Robert Alton and Gene Kelly
Photographed by Harry Stradling
Costumes supervised by Irene; designed by Tom Keogh
Film Editing by Blanche Sewell

CAST

Judy Garland (as Manuela), Gene Kelly, Walter Slezak, Gladys Cooper, Reginald Owen, George Zucco, The Nicholas Brothers, Lester Allen, Lola Deem, Ellen Ross, Mary Jo Ellis, Jean Dean, Marion Murray.

JUDY'S SONGS

You Can Do No Wrong
Mack The Black
Love Of My Life
Be A Clown
Voodoo (cut before release)

"Miss Garland dances in a trance, sings pleasantly and does a superb job of crockery smashing in the scene in which she discovers that her beloved pirate is only an itinerant mummer."
The New York Herald Tribune (Howard Barnes)

EASTER PARADE (1948) - MGM Techicolor
    Produced by Arthur Freed
    Associate Producer Roger Edens
    Directed by Charles Walters
    Screenplay by Sidney Sheldon, Frances Goodrich and Albert Hackett
    Original Story by Frances Goodrich and Albert Hackett
    Songs by Irving Berlin
    Musical Direction by Johnny Green
    Orchestrations by Conrad Salinger, Mason Van Cleave and Leo Arnaud
    Vocal Arrangements by Robert Tucker
    Costumes by Irene
    Photographed by Harry Stradling
    Musical Numbers staged and directed by Robert Alton
    Film Editing by Albert Akst
    CAST
        Judy Garland (as Hannah Brown), Fred Astaire, Peter Lawford, Ann Miller, Clinton Sundberg, Jules
        Munshin, Jeni LeGon, Jimmy Bates, Richard Beavers, Dick Simmons, Dee Turnell, Lola Albright, Joi
        Lansing.
    JUDY'S SONGS
        Better Luck Next Time
        Michigan
        It Only Happens When I Dance With You
        A Fella With An Umbrella
        I Love A Piano
        When That Midnight Choo Choo Leaves For Alabam'
        Ragtime Violin
        Snookey Ookums
        A Couple of Swells
        Easter Parade
        Mr. Monotony (cut before release)

        *"Irving Berlin, Fred Astaire and Judy Garland have pooled their musical and dancing talents in a smart
        and fetching screen carnival . . . Miss Garland has matured to a remarkable degree in "Easter Parade".
        . . a handsome and knowing actress. Her latest film performance is altogether her best."*
                        The New York Herald Tribune (Howard Barnes)

WORDS AND MUSIC (1948) - MGM Technicolor
    Produced by Arthur Freed
    Directed by Norman Taurog
    Screenplay by Fred Finklehoffe
    Story by Guy Bolton and Jean Holloway
    Adaptation by Ben Feiner, Jr.
    Songs by Richard Rodgers and Lorenz Hart
    Musical Direction by Lennie Hayton
    Orchestrations by Conrad Salinger
    Vocal Arrangements by Robert Tucker
    Musical Numbers staged and choreographed by Robert Alton
    Photographed by Charles Rosher and Harry Stradling
    Costumes by Helen Rose
    Film Editing by Albert Akst and Ferris Webster
    CAST
        Perry Como, Mickey Rooney, Ann Sothern, Tom Drake, Betty Garrett, Janet Leigh, Marshall
        Thompson, Jeanette Nolan, Richard Quine, Clinton Sundberg, Cyd Charisse, Harry Antrim, Ilka
        Gruning.
    GUEST STARS
        Judy Garland, June Allyson, Lena Horne, Gene Kelly, Vera Ellen, The Blackburn Twins, Allyn Ann
        McLerie, John Butler, Dee Turnell, Mel Torme.
    JUDY'S SONGS
        Johnny One Note
        I Wish I Were In Love Again

        *"The songs are as wonderful as ever, whether they are sung by Lena Horne, Perry Como, June
        Allyson and Judy Garland, or danced by Gene Kelly and Vera Ellen in an effective screen
        reproduction of "Slaughter On Tenth Avenue."*
                        The New York Herald Tribune (Howard Barnes)

IN THE GOOD OLD SUMMERTIME (1949) - MGM Technicolor

Produced by Joseph Pasternak
Directed by Robert Z. Leonard
Screenplay by Albert Hackett, Frances Goodrich and Ivan Tors
Based on a scenario by Samson Raphaelson
From the play "The Shop Around The Corner" by Miklos Laszlo
Musical Numbers directed by Robert Alton
Music direction by George Stoll
Photographed by Harry Stradling
Film Editing by Adrienne Fazan

CAST

Judy Garland (as Veronica Fisher), Van Johnson, S.Z. Sakall, Spring Byington, Buster Keaton, Marcia Van Dyke, Clinton Sundberg, Lillian Randolph, Ralph Sanford, Liza Minnelli.

JUDY'S SONGS

I Don't Care
Merry Christmas
Play That Barbershop Chord
Put Your Arms Around Me, Honey
Meet Me Tonight In Dreamland
In The Good Old Summertime
Last Night When We Were Young (cut before release)

"Looking much sturdier than she did in her last screen appearance, Judy performs the role of the ambitious heroine with some of her old times verve. She also sings the title song and several old favorites with unusual effectiveness."

The New York Daily News (Kate Cameron)

SUMMER STOCK (1950) - MGM Technicolor

Produced by Joseph Pasternak
Directed by Charles Walters
Screenplay by George Wells and Sy Gomberg
Musical Direction by Johnny Green and Saul Chaplin
Orchestrations by Conrad Salinger and Skip Martin
Dances Staged by Nick Castle
Photographed by Robert Planck
Costumes by Walter Plunkett
Film Editing by Albert Akst

CAST

Judy Garland (as Jane Falbury), Gene Kelly, Eddie Bracken, Gloria DeHaven, Marjorie Main, Phil Silvers, Carleton Carpenter, Ray Collins, Nita Bieber, Hans Conried.

JUDY'S SONGS

Get Happy
Friendly Star
Happy Harvest
If You Feel Like Singing
You Wonderful You

"Though the show's only distinguished song is an old one, "Get Happy", her voice and showmanlike delivery do wonders for the whole score."

Time Magazine

A STAR IS BORN (1954), A Warner Bros. Release, A Transcona Enterprises Prod.
>Produced by Sidney Luft
>Associate Producer Vernon Alves
>Directed by George Cukor
>Screenplay by Moss Hart
>Based on a screenplay by Dorothy Parker, Alan Campbell and
>>Robert Carson
>
>Story by William A. Wellman and Robert Carson
>Songs by Harold Arlen and Ira Gershwin
>*"Born in a Trunk"* number by Leonard Gershe
>Musical Direction by Ray Heindorf
>Dances by Richard Barstow
>Costumes by Irene Sharaff and Jean Louis
>Vocal Arrangemens by Jack Cathcart
>Orchestrations by Skip Martin
>Photographed by Same Leavitt
>Film Editing by Folmer Blangsted
>CAST
>>Judy Garland (as Esther Blodgett [Vicki Lester]), James Mason, Jack Carson, Charles Bickford, Tommy Noonan, Lucy Marlowe, Amanda Blake, Irving Bacon, Percy Helton, Joan Shawlee, Hazel Shermet, Lotus Robb, Nancy Kulp, Louis Jean Jeydt, Grady Sutton, Richard Webb.
>
>JUDY'S SONGS

The Man Tha Got Away	*I'll Get By*
Gotta Have Me Go With You	*You Took Advantage Of Me*
It's A New World	*The Peanut Vendor*
Someone At Last	*Swanee*
Born In A Trunk	*Here's What I'm Here For* (cut after release)
My Melancholy Baby	*Lose That Long Face* (cut after release)

"She gives what is just about the greatest one-woman show in modern movie history."

Time Magazine

PEPE (1960) - Columbia (CinemaScope and Eastman Color)
>Produced and Directed by George Sidney
>Associate Producer Jacques Gelman
>Screenplay by Dorothy Kingsley and Claude Binyon
>Based on a play by L. Bush-Fekete
>Story by Leonard Spigelgass and Sonya Levien
>Music Supervision and Background Score by Johnny Green
>Choreography by Eugene Loring and Alex Romero
>Gowns by Edith Head
>Photography by Joe MacDonald
>Film Editing by Viola Lawrence and Al Clark
>CAST
>>Cantinflas, Dan Dailey, Shirley Jones, Carlos Montalban, Ernie Kovacs, Jay North, Vicki Trickett, Matt Mattox, William Demarest, Michael Callan, Hank Henry, Suzanne Lloyd, Lela Bliss, Ray Walker.
>
>GUEST STARS
>>Maurice Chevalier, Bing Crosby, Richard Conte, Bobby Darin, Sammy Davis Jr., Jimmy Durante, Zsa Zsa Gabor, Greer Garson, Hedda Hopper, Joey Bishop, Peter Lawford, Janet Leigh, Jack Lemmon, Kim Novak, Donna Reed, Debbie Reynolds, Edward G. Robinson, Cesar Romero, Frank Sinatra, Ann B. Davis, Billie Burke, Dean Martin, Charles Coburn, Tony Curtis, Carlos Rivas, and The Voice of Judy Garland.
>
>JUDY'S SONGS
>>*The Faraway Part of Town,* by André Previn and Dory Langdon, was nominated for an Academy Award. Shirley Jones and Dan Dailey danced to the song sung by Judy on the soundtrack.
>
>*"Shirley Jones, Dan Dailey, Maurice Chevalier, Edward G. Robinson and the singing voice of Judy Garland are among the many talented casualties of this 1960 disaster."*

Judith Crist

JUDGMENT AT NUREMBERG (1961) - United Artists
Produced and Directed by Stanley Kramer
Associate Producer Phillip Langner
Screenplay by Abby Mann, based on his television script
Production designed by Rudolph Sternad
Music by Ernest Gold
Photographed by Ernest Laszlo
Costumes by Joe King
Film Editing by Fred Knudston
CAST
> Spencer Tracy, Burt Lancaster, Richard Widmark, Marlene Dietrich, Maximilian Schell, Judy Garland (as Irene Hoffman), Montgomery Clift, William Shatner, Edward Binns, Virginia Christine, Alan Baxter, Kenneth MacKenna, Werner Klemperer, Sheila Bromley, Karl Swenson, Ray Teal, Martin Brandt, Olga Fabian, John Wengraf, Howard Caine

"A fat young hausfrau, whom Judy Garland makes amazingly real tell(s) a horrifying tale of trumped-up charges of "racial contamination" against an elderly Jew."
The New York Times (B. Crowther)

A CHILD IS WAITING (1962) - A United Artists Release, A Stanley Kramer Production
Produced by Stanley Kramer
Associate Producer, Phillip Langner
Directed by John Cassavetes
Screenplay by Abby Mann, based on his television play.
Music by Ernest Gold
Photographed by Joseph LaShelle
Film Editing by Gene Fowler Jr.
CAST
> Burt Lancaster, Judy Garland (as Jean Hansen), Gena Rowlands, Steven Hill, Bruce Ritchey, Gloria McGehee, Paul Stewart, Elizabeth Wilson, Barbara Pepper, June Walker, Lawrence Tierney.

"Wonderful . . . is the way Judy Garland and Burt Lancaster work along with the children. Miss Garland and Lancaster radiate a warmth so genuine that one is certain that the children are responding directly to them, not merely following some vaguely comprehended script."
Saturday Review

GAY PURR-EE (1962) - A Warner Bros. Release, A UPA Production
Executive Producer Henry G. Saperstein
Associate Producer Lee Orgel
Directed by Abe Leviton
Screenplay by Dorothy and Chuck Jones
Songs by Harold Arlen and E.Y. Harburg
Music Arranged and Conducted by Mort Lindsey
Vocal Arrangements by Joseph J. Lilley
Photography by Roy Hutchcroft, Dan Miller, Jack Stevens and
    Duane Keegan
Art Direction by Victor Haboush
Film Editing by Ted Baker

A full-length animated feature with the voices of:
Judy Garland (as Mewsette), Robert Goulet, Hermione Gingold, Red Buttons, Morey Amsterdam, Paul Frees, Mel Blanc, Julie Bennett, Joan Gardner.
JUDY'S SONGS
Paris Is A Lonely Town
Take My Hand, Paree
Roses Red, Violets Blue
Little Drops Of Rain
The Mewsette Finais

". . . Judy Garland and Robert Goulet singing the Harold Arlen songs (pay particular attention to the lovely "Little Drops of Rain") are worth a constant ear."
Judith Crist

I COULD GO ON SINGING (1963) - United Artists, A Barbican Production, Panavision - Eastman Color
Produced by Stuart Millar and Lawrence Turman
Directed by Ronald Neame
Screenplay by Mayo Simon
Story by Robert Dozier
Musical Supervision by Saul Chaplin
Music by Mort Lindsey
Costumes by Edith Head
Photography by Arthur Ibbetson
New Songs by Harold Arlen and E.Y. Harburg
Film Editing by John Shirley
CAST
Judy Garland (as Jenny Bowman), Dirk Bogarde, Jack Klugman, Gregory Phillips, Aline MacMahon, Pauline Jameson, Jeremy Brunham, Russell Waters, Gerald Sim, Leon Cortez.
JUDY'S SONGS
I Could Go On Singing
Hello Bluebird
It Never Was You
By Myself
I Am The Monarch Of The Sea

"Miss Garland is - as always - real, the voice throbbing, the eyes aglow, the delicate features yielding to the demands of the years - the legs still long and lovely."
The New York Herald Tribune (Judith Crist)

JUDY GARLAND'S MOST FAMOUS CONCERTS

The Philadelphia Orchestra	July 10, 1943
The Palladium, London	April 14, 1951
	June 25, 1951
The Palace, New York City	October 16, 1951
Los Angeles Philharmonic	April 26, 1952
The Curran, San Francisco	June 4, 1952
The Palladium, London	November 18, 1954
The Palace, New York City	September 26, 1956
The Metropolitian Opera House, New York City	May 11, 1959
The Palladium, London	August 28, 1960
	September 4, 1960
	December 1, 1960
Carnegie Hall, New York City	April 23, 1961
The Palladium, London	July 23, 1964
	November 8, 1964
	November 16, 1964
Westbury Music Fair, Long Island	July, 1967
The Palace, New York City	August 18, 1967
Garden State Arts Center, New Jersey	June 25, 1968

----And 100 more!

JUDY GARLAND ON TELEVISION

THE FORD STAR JUBILEE Sept. 24, 1955. CBS.

Judy's Songs: "You Made Me Love You", "Swanee", "It's De-Lovely", "While We're Young", "But Not For Me", "For Me And My Gal", "The Boy Next Door", "The Trolley Song", "Rockabye Your Baby", "A Couple of Swells" (with David Wayne) and "Over The Rainbow."

THE GENERAL ELECTRIC THEATRE April 8, 1956. CBS.

Judy's Songs: "Last Night When We Were Young", "I Feel A Song Comin' On", "April Showers", "Life Is Just A Bowl Of Cherries", "Dirty Hands, Dirty Face" and "Maybe I'll Come Back".

THE JUDY GARLAND SHOW Feb. 25, 1962. CBS.

Judy's Songs: "Just In Time", "The Man That Got Away", "When You're Smiling", "I Can't Give You Anything But Love", "You Made Me Love You", "The Trolley Song", "Swanee", "Rockabye Your Baby," "San Francisco", "You Do Something To Me" (with Frank Sinatra and Dean Martin), "Let There Be Love" and "You're Nobody Till Somebody Loves You" (with Sinatra and Martin).

THE JACK PAAR SHOW December, 1962. NBC.

Judy's Songs: "Paris Is A Lonely Town", "Little Drops of Rain" and "Mewsette" (with Robert Goulet).

JUDY AND HER GUESTS March, 1963. CBS.

Judy's Songs: "I Happen To Like New York", "Through The Years", "Hello Bluebird", "Here I'll Stay" (with Robert Goulet), "Get Happy", "By Myself", "This Can't Be Love", "Love Is A Lovely Thing" (with Robert Goulet), "Almost Like Being In Love" and "I Could Go On Singing".

SUNDAY NIGHT AT THE PALLADIUM (British TV) March, 1963.

Judy's Songs: "Almost Like Being In Love", "Comes Once in A Lifetime", "This Can't Be Love", "I Could Go On Singing" and "Smile".

(Parts of this show were televised on The Ed Sullivan Show later in March, 1963 on CBS.)

THE JUDY GARLAND SHOW Sept. 29, 1963. CBS.

Judy's Songs: "Call Me Irresponsible", "Chicago", "Fly Me To The Moon", two Medleys with Donald O'Connor, and "Maybe I'll Come Back".

THE JUDY GARLAND SHOW Oct. 6, 1963. CBS.

Judy's Songs: "Just In Time", "Comes Once In A Lifetime", "Happy Days Are Here Again","Get Happy" (with Barbra Streisand), "There's No Business Like Show Business" (with Streisand and Ethel Merman), "Happy Harvest" (with Streisand), a medley with Streisand, "You Made Me Love You", "The Trolley Song" and "Maybe I'll Come Back".

THE JUDY GARLAND SHOW Oct. 13, 1963. CBS.

Judy's Songs: "A Foggy Day", "The Man That Got Away", "Day In Day Out" (with Lena Horne), "Mad Dogs And Englishmen" (with Lena Horne and Terry-Thomas), a medley with Lena Horne, and "Maybe I'll Come Back".

THE JUDY GARLAND SHOW Oct. 20, 1963. CBS.

Judy's Songs: "Swanee", "Alexander's Ragtime Band", "Y'all Come", "I Wish You Love", "Side By Side" (with George Maharis), "Take Me Out To The Ball Game" (with Leo Durocher), and "Maybe I'll Come Back".

THE JUDY GARLAND SHOW Oct. 27, 1963. CBS.

Judy's Songs: "Life Is Just A Bowl Of Cherries", "Happiness Is A Thing Called Joe", "San Francisco", "The Doodlin' Song" (with June Allyson), a medley with Steve Lawrence and June Allyson, and "Maybe I'll Come Back".

THE JUDY GARLAND SHOW Nov. 3, 1963. CBS.

Judy's Songs: "Smile", "Rockabye Your Baby", "My Bill", "Moon River", "From This Moment On", "Getting To Know You" (with Zina Bethune), a "Porgy and Bess" medley with Vic Damone, a medley with Zina Bethune and Vic Damone, and "Maybe I'll Come Back".

THE JUDY GARLAND SHOW Nov. 10, 1963. CBS.

Judy's Songs: "I've Got My Love To Keep Me Warm", "Hey, Look Me Over", "Memories of You" (with Count Basie), "A Cottage For Sale", "April In Paris" (with Mel Torme), "The Sweetest Sounds/Strike Up The Band" (with Count Basie) and "Maybe I'll Come Back".

THE JUDY GARLAND SHOW Nov. 17, 1963. CBS.

Judy's Songs: "Liza", "Come Rain Or Come Shine", a medley with Liza Minnelli, "As Long As He Needs Me", "Let Me Entertain You" (with Minnelli), "Two Lost Souls" (with Minnelli) and "Maybe I'll Come Back" (with Minnelli).

THE JUDY GARLAND SHOW Dec. 1, 1963. CBS.

Judy's Songs: "When You're Smiling", "I Love Bein' Here With You" (with Peggy Lee), "How About Me", a medley with Jack Carter, "It's A Good Day", "Never Will I Marry", a medley with Peggy Lee, and "Maybe I'll Come Back".

THE JUDY GARLAND SHOW Dec, 8, 1963. CBS.

Judy's Songs: "I Feel A Song Comin' On", "Too Late Now", "Who Cares", "When The Sun Comes Out", "Ol' Man River", a medley with Mickey Rooney from their films, and "Maybe I'll Come Back".

THE JUDY GARLAND SHOW Dec. 15, 1963. CBS.

Judy's Songs: "Stormy Weather", "One For My Baby", "That's All", "My Buddy" (with Dick Shawn), "Yes, Indeed" (with Tony Bennett and Dick Shawn), a medley with Tony Bennett, and "Maybe I'll Come Back".

THE JUDY GARLAND SHOW Dec. 22, 1963. CBS.

Judy's Songs: "Have Yourself A Merry Little Christmas", "Little Drops Of Rain", "Jingle Bells" (with Jack Jones), "Winter Wonderland", "Sleigh Ride" (with Jack Jones and Liza Minnelli), "The Christmas Song" (with Mel Torme), "Consider Yourself" (with her children Liza Minnelli, Lorna and Joe Luft), "Deck The Halls" (with everyone), and "Over The Rainbow".

THE JUDY GARLAND SHOW Dec. 29, 1963. CBS.

Judy's Songs: "Hello Bluebird", "If Love Were All", "Zing! Went The Strings Of My Heart", "Do It Again", "Get Me To The Church On Time", "More", a medley with Bobby Darin, and "Maybe I'll Come Back".

THE JUDY GARLAND SHOW Jan. 5, 1964. CBS.

Judy's Songs: "Through The Years", "Here's That Rainy Day", "This Could Be The Start Of Something Big", a medley with Steve Allen, "The Party's Over" (with Mel Torme), "Island In the West Indies", a medley with Steve Allen and Mel Torme, and "Maybe I'll Come Back".

THE JUDY GARLAND SHOW Jan. 12, 1964. CBS.

Judy's Songs: "A Pretty Girl Milking Her Cow", "Puttin' On The Ritz", "Everybody's Doing It" and "Let's Do It" (with Ethel Merman, Shelly Berman and Peter Gennaro), a medley with Ethel Merman, "Shenandoah" and "The Battle Hymn Of The Republic".

THE JUDY GARLAND SHOW Jan 19, 1964. CBS.

Judy's Songs: "By Myself", "Better Luck Next Time", "Almost Like Being In Love", "This Can't Be Love", "I Believe In You" (with Chita Rivera), "They Can't Take That Away From Me", a "West Side Story" medley with Vic Damone, and "Maybe I'll Come Back".

THE JUDY GARLAND SHOW Jan. 26, 1964. CBS.

Judy's Songs: "The Boy Next Door", "All Alone", "I'm Old Fashioned", "Seventy-Six Trombones", a "Glenn Miller Medley" with Martha Raye, and "Oh, Lord! I'm On My Way".

THE JUDY GARLAND SHOW Feb. 2, 1964. CBS.

Judy's Songs: "San Francisco", "Paris Is A Lonely Town", "Smoke Gets In Your Eyes", "Some Of These Days", "Whispering" (with The Kirby Stone Four), a children's medley with Louis Jourdan, "What'll I Do", and "The Battle Hymn Of The Republic".

THE JUDY GARLAND SHOW Feb. 9, 1964. CBS.

Judy's Songs: "Liza", "Lorna", "Happiness Is A Thing Called Joe", "That's Entertainment", "Rockabye Your Baby", "Swing Low, Sweet Chariot", "He's Got The Whole World In His Hands", "Make Someone Happy", a World War I medley, and "America The Beautiful".

THE JUDY GARLAND SHOW Feb. 16, 1964. CBS.

Judy's Songs: "Alone Together", "Come Rain Or Come Shine", "A Stranger In Town", "After You've Gone", "Smile", "Great Day", "The Trolley Song" (with Mel Torme), a medley with Diahann Carroll, and "Don't Ever Leave Me".

THE JUDY GARLAND SHOW Feb. 23, 1964. CBS.

Judy's Songs: "Swanee", "Just In Time," "Last Night When We Were Young", "Almost Like Being In Love", "This Can't Be Love", "If Love Were All", "A Foggy Day", "When The Sun Comes Out", "Just You, Just Me", and a Palace medley with Jack Jones.

THE JUDY GARLAND SHOW March 1, 1964. CBS.

Judy's Songs: "Hello Bluebird", "If Love Were All", "Zing! Went The Strings Of My Heart", "Some People", "When Your Lover Has Gone", "I've Got A Lot Of Livin' To Do", "On The Sunny Side Of The Street", a "Wizard of Oz" medley with Ray Bolger and Jane Powell, and "Maybe I'll Come Back".

THE JUDY GARLAND SHOW March 8, 1964. CBS.

Judy's Songs: "The Man That Got Away", "I Feel A Song Comin' On", "Toot Toot Tootsie", "Love Of My Life", "The Boy Next Door", "On The Atchison, Topeka And The Santa Fe", "You're Nearer", "Be A Clown", "Steppin' Out With My Baby", "I'm Always Chasing Rainbows", "If I Had a Talking Picture Of You", "Dirty Hands, Dirty Face", "I'm Nobody's Baby", "Alexander's Ragtime Band" and "Comes Once In A Lifetime".

THE JUDY GARLAND SHOW March 15, 1964. CBS.

Judy's Songs: "Chicago", "Lucky Day", "Sweet Danger", "I Love You", "Do I Love You", "Old Devil Moon", "Never Will I Marry", "When Your Lover Has Gone", "Down With Love", "Any Place I Hang My Hat Is Home", a "Kismet" medley with Vic Damone, and "Lost In The Stars".

THE JUDY GARLAND SHOW March 22, 1964. CBS.

Judy's Songs: "Get Happy", "I Am Loved", "Comes Once In A Lifetime", "Life Is Just A Bowl Of Cherries", "Why Can't I?", "Joey, Joey, Joey", "Love", "Sail Away", "As Long As He Needs Me", "I've Got A Right To Sing The Blues", "Poor Butterfly" (with The Robert Cole Trio), and "Ol' Man River".

THE JUDY GARLAND SHOW March 29, 1964. CBC.

Judy's Songs: "After You've Gone", "When You're Smiling", "By Myself", "Just In Time", "If Love Were All", "Just You, Just Me", "The Nearness Of You", "Time After Time", "That Old Feeling", "Carolina In The Morning", "Almost Like Being In Love", "This Can't Be Love" "The Last Dance", "Suppertime", "A Foggy Day" and "When The Sun Comes Out".

THE JACK PAAR SHOW December, 1964. NBC.

Judy's Songs: "Never Will I Marry" and "What Now, My Love".

JUDY AND LIZA, LIVE, AT THE LONDON PALLADIUM Dec. 1964 (British TV)

Judy's Songs: "Just Once In A Lifetime", "The Man That Got Away", "Hello Liza, Hello Mama" (with Liza Minnelli), "Together" (with Liza), a medley with Liza, "The Music That Makes Me Dance", "Get Happy/Happy Days Are Here Again" (with Liza), "He's Got The Whole World In His Hands" (with Liza), "San Francisco", "Over The Rainbow", and "Chicago" (with Liza).

ON BROADWAY TONIGHT Feb. 1965. NBC.

Judy's Songs: "When You're Smiling", "Almost Like Being In Love/This Can't Be Love", "I Wish You Love" (with The Allen Brothers), "The Music That Makes Me Dance" and "Rockabye Your Baby".

THE ACADEMY AWARDS SHOW April, 1965. ABC.

Judy sang a special tribute to Cole Porter, a medley of his songs, "I Get A Kick Out Of You", "Don't Fence Me In", "Night And Day", "I Love You", "Let's Do It" and "You're The Top".

THE ANDY WILLIAMS SHOW Sept. 1965. NBC.

Judy's Songs: "On A Wonderful Day Like Today" (with Andy Williams), "Get Happy", a medley with Andy Williams, and "The Man That Got Away".

THE ED SULLIVAN SHOW Oct. 1965. CBS.

Judy's Songs: "Come Rain Or Come Shine", "By Myself" and "Rockabye Your Baby".

THE HOLLYWOOD PALACE (Judy as hostess) Nov. 1965. ABC.

Judy's Songs: "Just Once In A Lifetime", a "West Side Story" medley with Vic Damone, "A Couple Of Swells", "I Loved Him" and "The Palace Medley" "Some Of These Days", "My Man", "I Don't Care" and "Shine On, Harvest Moon".

THE PERRY COMO SHOW Feb. 1966. NBC.

Judy's Songs: "What Now, My Love", "Just In Time", "If You Feel Like Singing, Sing" (with Perry Como), "It's A Grand Night For Singing" (with Perry Como), "My Baby's Lovin' Arms" (with Perry Como), a medley with Como, and "Side By Side" (with Perry Como and Bill Cosby).

THE SAMMY DAVIS SHOW March, 1966. NBC.

Judy's Songs: "When You're Smiling", "The Man That Got Away", "Give My Regards To Broadway", and a medley with Sammy Davis, Jr.

THE SAMMY DAVIS SHOW March, 1966. NBC.

Judy's Songs: "Almost Like Being In Love/This Can't Be Love" and a medley with Sammy Davis, Jr.

THE MIKE DOUGLAS SHOW July, 1968. Syndicated

Judy's Songs: "For Once In My Life", "How Insensitive", "Blue Skies" (with Peter Lawford) and "Over The Rainbow".

THE DICK CAVETT SHOW Dec. 1968. ABC.

Judy's Song: "God Bless Johnny".

THE JOHNNY CARSON SHOW Dec. 1968. NBC.

Judy's Songs: "All For You" and "Till After The Holidays".

THE MERV GRIFFIN SHOW Dec., 1968. CBS.

Judy's Songs: "Have Yourself A Merry Little Christmas", "The Trolley Song" and "I'd Like To Hate Myself In The Morning".

THE MERV GRIFFIN SHOW Dec, 1968. CBS.

Judy's Songs: "Just In Time" and "If You Were The Only Boy In The World" (with Arthur Treacher).

SUNDAY NIGHT AT THE PALLADIUM Feb, 1969. (British TV)

Judy's Songs: "Get Happy", "For Once In My Life" and "I Belong To London".

JUDY GARLAND DISCOGRAPHY

SINGLES (in alphabetical order)

All God's Chillun Got Rhythm/Everybody Sing	Decca 1432	1937
Aren't You Kinda' Glad We Did? (with Dick Haymes)/For You, For Me, Forevermore	Decca 23460	1946
Be A Clown	MGM 30097	1948
Better Luck Next Time	MGM 30187	1948
Bidin' My Time/I Got Rhythm	Decca 23310	1943
(The) Birthday of a King/Star of the East	Decca 4050	1940
	Decca 23658	
	Decca 9-2368	
Blues in the Night	Decca 4081	1941
(The) Boy Next Door/Have Yourself a Merry Little Christmas	Decca 23362	1944
(The) Boy Next Door/Smilin' Through	Decca 9-29296	1945
Boys and Girls Like You and Me/(The) Trolley Song	Decca 23361	1944
Buds Won't Bud/I'm Nobody's Baby	Decca 3174	1940
But Not for Me	Decca 23309	1943
By Myself/It's Lovely to Be Back Again in London	EMI-CL 14791 (U.K.)	1957
Changing My Tune	Decca 23688	1946
Chicago/San Francisco	Capitol 6125	1961
Connecticut/Mine (with Bing Crosby)	Decca 23804	1945
Come Rain or Come Shine/Rockabye My Baby	Capitol 6127	1961
Comes Once in a Lifetime/Sweet Danger	Capitol 4656	1962
Could You Use Me?/Embraceable You	Decca 23303	1943
(A) Couple of Swells/Medley (with Fred Astaire)	MGM 30186	1948
Cry, Baby, Cry/Sleep, My Baby, Sleep	Decca 1796	1938
(Dear Mr. Gable) You Made Me Love You/You Can't Have Everything	Decca 1463	1937
Dear Mr. Gable/Over the Rainbow	MGM-KGC 166	1939
	Decca 2-3962	
	Decca 9-23961	
Don't Tell Me That Story/There Is No Breeze	Decca 23746	1946
Easter Parade/A Fella with an Umbrella (with Peter Lawford)	MGM 30185	1948
(The) End of the Rainbow	Decca 3231	1940
Embraceable You/Swanee	Decca 2881	1939
Embraceable You/Could You Use Me?	Decca 23303	1943
Everybody Sing	Decca 1332	1937
Everybody Sing/All God's Chillun Got Rhythm	Decca 1432	1937
F.D.R. Jones/How About You?	Decca 4072	1941
Fascinatin' Rhythm/Zing! Went the Strings of My Heart	Decca 18543	1939
(A) Fella with an Umbrella (with Peter Lawford)/Easter Parade	MGM 30185	1948
Figaro/Oceans Apart	Brunswick 2953 (U.K.)	1939
For Me and My Gal/When You Wore a Tulip (with Gene Kelly)	Decca 18480	1942
	Decca 9-25115	
	Decca 25115	
Fou You, For Me, Forevermore/Aren't You Kinda' Glad We Did? (with Dick Haymes)	Decca 23460	1946
Friendly Star/Get Happy	MGM 30254	1950
	MGM 30254	
Friendship (with Johnny Mercer)/Wearing of the Green	Decca 3/65	1940
Get Happy/Friendly Star	MGM 30254	1950
	MGM 30254	
Go Home, Joe/Heartbroken	Columbia 40023	1954
Happy Harvest/If You Feel Like Singing	MGM 3025	1950
Have Yourself a Merry Little Christmas/(The) Boy Next Door	Decca 23362	1944
Have Yourself a Merry Little Christmas/You'll Never Walk Alone	Decca 9-29295	1945

Heartbroken/Go Home, Joe	Columbia 40023	1954
Here's What I'm Here For/(The) Man That Got Away	Columbia 40270	1954
He's Got the Whole World in His Hands (with Liza Minnelli)/Hello, Dolly	Capitol 5497	1964
Hello, Bluebird/I Could Go On Singing	Capitol 4938	1962
Hello, Dolly!/He's Got the Whole World in His Hands (with Liza Minnelli)	Capitol 5497	1964
I Could Go On Singing/Hello, Bluebird	Capitol 4938	1962
I Don't Care/Play That Barbershop Chord	MGM 50026	1949
I Got Rhythm/Bidin' My Time	Decca 23310	1943
I May Be Wrong/Over the Rainbow	V-Disc 335A	1943
I Never Knew/On the Sunny Side of the Street	Decca 18524	1942
I Wish I Were in Love Again/Nothing But You	Decca 24469	1946
I Wish I Were in Love Again/Johnny One Note	MGM 30172	1948
If I Had You/On the Atchison, Topeka and the Santa Fe (with The Merry Macs)	Decca 23436	1945
If You Feel Like Singing/Happy Harvest	MGM 3025	1950
I'm Always Chasing Rainbows/Our Love Affair	Decca 3593	1940
I'm Nobody's Baby/Buds Won't Bud	Decca 3174	1940
In Between/Sweet Sixteen	Decca 15045	1939
	Decca 29233	
	Decca 9-40219	
(In the Valley) When the Evening Sun Goes Down	Decca 23438	1945
It Never Rains But It Pours/Ten Pins in the Sky	Decca 2017	1938
	Brunswick 02656	
It's a Great Big World (with Virginia O'Brien)	Decca 23460	1945
It's a Great Day for the Irish/(A) Pretty Girl	Decca 3604	1940
	Decca 25043	
	Decca 9-25043	
It's Lovely to Be Back Again in London/By Myself	EMI-CL 14791 (U.K.)	1957
(The) Jitterbug/Over the Rainbow	Decca 2762	1939
Johnny One Note/I Wish I Were in Love Again	MGM 30172	1948
(A) Journey to a Star/No Love, No Nothin'	Decca 18484	1943
Last Call for Love/Poor You	Decca 18320	1941
Little Drops of Rain/Paris Is a Lonely Town	Warner Bros. 5310	1962
Look for the Silver Lining	MGM 30002	1946
Look for the Silver Lining	MGM 30431	1946
	MGM 30212	
Love of My Life/You Can Do No Wrong	MGM 30098	1948
Mack the Black	MGM 30099	1948
(The) Man That Got Away/Here's What I'm Here For	Columbia 40270	1954
(The) Man That Got Away	Capitol 6126	1961
Maybe I'll Come Back/Over the Rainbow	Capitol 6128	1955-56
Medley (with Fred Astaire)/(A) Couple of Swells	MGM 30186	1948
Meet Me in St. Louis/Skip to My Lou	Decca 23360	1944
Meet Me in St. Louis/(The) Trolley Song	Decca 25494	1944
	Decca 9-25494	
Meet Me Tonight in Dreamland/Put Your Arms Around Me, Honey	MGM 50025	1949
Merry Christmas	MGM 30212	1949
Mine (with Bing Crosby)/Connecticut	Decca 23804	1945
No Love, No Nothin'/(A) Journey to a Star	Decca 18484	1943
Nothing But You/ I Wish I Were in Love Again	Decca 24469	1946
Oceans Apart/Figaro	Brunswick 2953 (U.K)	1939
On the Atchison, Topeka and the Santa Fe (with the Merry Macs)/If I Had You	Decca 23436	1945
On the Sunny Side of the Street/I Never Knew	Decca 18524	1942
Our Love Affair/I'm Always Chasing Rainbows	Decca 3593	1940
Over the Rainbow/(The) Jitterbug	Decca 2762	1939
Over the Rainbow/(Dear Mr. Gable) You Made Me Love You	MGM-KGC 166	1939
	Decca 2-3962	
	Decca 9-23961	

Over the Rainbow/I May Be Wrong	V-Disc 335A	1943
Over the Rainbow/Maybe I'll Come Back	Capitol 6128	1955-56
Paris Is a Lonely Town/Little Drops of Rain	Warner Bros. 5310	1962
Play That Barbershop Chord/I Don't Care	MGM 50026	1949
Poor Little Rich Girl/That Old Black Magic	Decca 18540	1942
Poor You/Last Call for Love	Decca 18320	1941
(A) Pretty Girl/It's a Great Day for the Irish	Decca 3604	1940
	Decca 25043	
	Decca 9-25043	
Put Your Arms Around Me, Honey/Meet Me Tonight in Dreamland	MGM 50025	1949
Rockabye My Baby/Zing! Went the Strings of My Heart	Capitol 4624	1961
Rockabye My Baby/Come Rain or Come Shine	Capitol 6127	1961
Round and Round	Decca 23459	1945
San Francisco/Chicago	Capitol 6125	1961
Send My Baby Back to Me/Without a Memory	Columbia 40010	1954
Sleep, My Baby, Sleep/Cry, Baby, Cry	Decca 1796	1938
Skip to My Lou/Meet Me in St. Louis	Decca 23360	1944
Smilin' Through/(The) Boy Next Door	Decca 9-29296	1945
Smilin' Through/You'll Never Walk Alone	Decca 23539	1945
	Decca 9-23539	
Star of the East/(The) Birthday of a King	Decca 4050	1940
	Decca 23658	
	Decca 9-2368	
Stompin' at the Savoy/Swing Mr. Charlie	Decca 848	1936
Swanee/Embraceable You	Decca 2881	1939
Swanee/That's Entertainment	Capitol 6129	1961
Sweet Danger/Comes Once in a Lifetime	Capitol 4656	1962
Sweet Sixteen/In Between	Decca 15045	1939
	Decca 29233	
	Decca 9-40219	
Swing Mr. Charlie/Stompin' at the Savoy	Decca 848	1936
Ten Pins in the Sky/It Never Rains But It Pours	Decca 2017	1938
	Brunswick 02656	
That Old Black Magic/Poor Little Rich Girl	Decca 18540	1942
This Heart of Mine/Love	Decca 18660	1945
There Is No Breeze/Don't Tell Me That Story	Decca 23746	1946
That's Entertainment/Swanee	Capitol 6129	1961
(The) Trolley Song/Boys and Girls Like You and Me	Decca 23361	1944
(The) Trolley Song/Meet Me in St. Louis	Decca 25494	1944
	Decca 9-25494	
Wearing of the Green/Friendship (with Johnny Mercer)	Decca 3/65	1940
When You Wore a Tulip (with Gene Kelly)/For Me and My Gal	Decca 18480	1942
	Decca 9-25115	
	Decca 25115	
When the Evening Sun Goes Down (In the Valley)	Decca 23438	1945
Who?	MGM 30003	1946
Without a Memory/Send My Baby Back to me	Columbia 40010	1954
Yah-ta-ta/You've Got Me Where You Want Me (with Bing Crosby)	Decca 23410	1945
You Can Do No Wrong/Love of My Life	MGM 30098	1948
You Can't Have Everything/(Dear Mr. Gable) You Made Me Love You	Decca 1463	1937
You'll Never Walk Alone/Have Yourself a Merry Little Christmas	Decca 9-29295	1945
You'll Never Walk Alone/Smilin' Through	Decca 23539	1945
	Decca 9-23539	
You've Got Me Where You Want Me (with Bing Crosby)/Yah-ta-ta	Decca 23410	1945
Zing! When the Strings of My Heart/Fascinatin' Rhythm	Decca 18543	1939
Zing! When the Strings of My Heart/Rockabye My Baby	Capitol 4624	1961

ALBUMS (on Major Labels) – *As originally released*

CAPITOL RECORDS:

Miss Show Business
Judy
Alone
Judy in Love
Judy at Carnegie Hall
Garland At the Grove
The Letter
Judy, That's Entertainment
The Garland Touch
The Hits of Judy Garland
I Could Go On Singing
Just for Openers
Judy Garland and Liza Minnelli / Live at the Palladium
The Judy Garland Deluxe Set
Judy in London
Judy Garland - Liza Minnelli / Live at the London Palladium
Our Love Letter
Judy Garland
Los Hitos Del Hit Parade, Vol. 8
Greatest Hits of the 30's & 40's
World's Best Love Songs
Collector's Best - Ten Legendary Song Stylists
The Greatest Hits of the 30's
Greatest Artists of our Time: Dinah Shore / Judy Garland
The Stereo Collector's Set, Vol. 7
The Best of the Great Song Stylists
The Stereo Collector's Set, Vol. 2 -
   Broadway & Hollywood Showstoppers
Showstoppers
Broadway & Hollywood Showstoppers
Popular Gold Album
More Stars in Stereo
Hits of Judy Garland

COLUMBIA RECORDS:

A Star is Born
Judy Garland
A Star Is Born / House Party
A Star Is Born
Pepe

DECCA RECORDS:

The Wizard of Oz
The Judy Garland Souvenir Album
George Gershwin Songs, Vol. II
The Judy Garland Second Souvenir Album
Girl Crazy (with Mickey Rooney)
Meet Me in St. Louis
The Harvey Girls
The Judy Garland Third Souvenir Album
Judy Garland Sings (w/Dick Haymes & Gene Kelly)
Judy at the Palace
Girl Crazy
Judy Garland, Vol. II
The Magic of Judy Garland
Girl Crazy (with Mickey Rooney)
Judy at the Palace

DECCA RECORDS:	Judy Garland - Greatest Performances
	Selections from the Harvey Girls/
	Meet Me in St. Louis
	The Best of Judy Garland
	Judy Garland's Greatest Hits
	Collector's Items (1936-45)

DECCA RECORDS:

Judy Garland - Greatest Performances
Selections from the Harvey Girls/
   Meet Me in St. Louis
The Best of Judy Garland
Judy Garland's Greatest Hits
Collector's Items (1936-45)

MGM RECORDS:

Till the Clouds Roll By
The Pirate
Words and Music
Easter Parade
In the Good Old Summertime
Summer Stock
Merry Christmas
Judy Garland
Get Happy
Look for the Silver Lining
The Wizard of Oz
Judy Garland Sings
Till the Clouds Roll By / Gentlemen Prefer Blondes
The Pirate / Summer Stock
The Pirate / Les Girls
Easter Parade / Annie Get Your Gun
In the Good Old Summertime / An American in Paris
Judy Garland
The Wizard of Oz
The Judy Garland Story - The Star Years
The Judy Garland Story, Vol. II - The Hollywood Years
Magnificent Moments from MGM Movies
The Very Best of Motion Picture Musicals
The Very Best of Judy Garland
The Wizard of Oz
Judy Garland
Judy Garland in Song
Judy Garland - The Golden Archive Series
Judy Garland - The Golden Years at MGM
Forever Judy
The Wizard of Oz
Easter Parade / Singing in the Rain
The Pirate / Hit the Deck / Pagan Love Song
Born to Sing
The Wizard of Oz
The Pirate / Easter Parade
Judy Garland - The Hollywood Years